Marketing
yo
School

Margaret Spooner

FORBES PUBLICATIONS

Marketing your School

© Margaret Spooner 1996

Published by Forbes Publications Ltd
29 Bedford Street
London WC2E 9ED
Tel: 0171 379 1299   Fax: 0171 379 6740

All rights reserved
First published 1996
ISBN 1 899527 06 0

Printed in Great Britain
by St Edmundsbury Press, Suffolk

Contents

Chapter 1
Introduction

You probably trained as a teacher because you wanted to teach and, unless your subject is business studies, you may have little or no interest in marketing. However, recent developments in the world of education mean that marketing has become a necessity for all schools. In the new climate of change, you need to work hard to attract pupils to your school and, although you may be lucky enough to have some governors or parents with marketing expertise who can advise and help the school at present, they may not always be available. And, besides, the outcome is too important to leave to others. So you yourself need to understand the elements of marketing which can help you promote the school.

There are plenty of books about public relations and marketing, but many shroud the theory in so much jargon that reading them is a chore, and none specifically addresses the needs of schools and colleges. This book, then, is not a business book. It is intended as a practical manual which will help you to do your job, and, in particular, to achieve success in marketing your school.

The book will help head teachers, school governors and others involved in the marketing and promotion of schools deal with the new challenge they face: an increased need to market their schools but with limited resources. It explains the elements of marketing that are relevant to schools, in language that is, I hope, easy to understand.

Different categories of school have different needs, but the same basic marketing principles apply. Throughout the book there are practical examples, which can be adapted to your school, so you can use *Marketing Your School* as a useful aid whenever necessary. It is not necessary for everyone to read the book from cover to cover. If you are ultimately responsible for your school's marketing you may wish to read the book right through, but if you are only involved in one aspect of promoting the school you can turn to the chapter dealing with that topic to find guidelines and examples which will help you handle your school's needs.

What is marketing?

Marketing is the process of bringing together a buyer and a seller. A company wanting to sell its products will direct its marketing efforts toward finding buyers for its products, and ensuring that it continues to provide the type of products buyers want. Otherwise it will not make sales and the company will go out of business. Schools must make similar efforts to attract and keep pupils.

When you are offering what the customer wants, then you are marketing well. If your school is constantly oversubscribed, your marketing is undoubtedly working, and it is unlikely to be so effective simply by accident. You are making sure the pupils get a good education - in other words the product is right for your customers, the parents who want their children to attend your school. And their perception that the school is providing a good education suggests that you're promoting it well, probably by creating opportunities to impress outsiders with the benefits the school offers.

Product and promotion are two of the "four Ps" of classic marketing theory. The others are price and place. The four Ps are variables that marketing people use when planning the activities that will enable them to meet their objectives. If you were selling cosmetics you would need to consider the best outlets (the place) and the price to charge, both of which would depend on the image you created for the product. You would need to understand detailed theory and much of the jargon contained in marketing text books.

However in the education market, unless you are in the independent sector, price is not a factor in attracting pupils to the school. The place where the school is located is unlikely to change, and if it does teachers will probably not be involved in making the decision. Of course, location can be used as part of your promotion, for example if the school is easily reached by public transport or situated in idyllic surroundings. But, since few teachers influence the price and place of the education their school provides, *Marketing your School* only covers the two Ps within their control: product and promotion.

We have all observed marketing at work, often without realising it. The price and position of goods on a supermarket shelf; the 'junk' mail addressed to you as a potential buyer of specialist services; glossy brochures selling anything from houses and cars to life insurance; comments from company directors on the radio or in a newspaper, and of course advertising itself, all form part of somebody's marketing programme and are part of a carefully devised plan. Even the leaflet dropped through your letter box by the local builder or plumber is likely to produce more response if it is well timed to arrive in the spring when householders are planning external maintenance, or in the autumn when the central heating may be causing problems. Similarly, by deciding your marketing strategy and developing a marketing plan you can improve the effectiveness of your school's marketing. The marketing plan should form part of the school's overall plan for the coming year and command part of the budget.

Ideally, the planning stage for marketing activities should come before carrying them out, so you might reasonably expect Marketing your School to begin with a chapter on strategy and planning. However, it is only after you acquire an understanding of marketing activities that you can start to develop a marketing plan. You need to understand the market in which the school operates, and the tactics which are likely to be most successful in reaching customers. You need a knowledge of various methods of promotion, such as advertising and press relations. You need to know how to learn more about your market. Within the marketing plan you will need to describe your market, product, share of market, suggest how to improve market share, how to improve product, the cost of doing so, and a timetable for the planned activities. For this reason, market planning and strategy are the subject of the final chapter of the book, and the earlier chapters show you how to approach individual aspects of marketing so that you will have a thorough foundation for tackling your own plan when you reach chapter 10.

If you are not yet convinced of the need to plan consider these examples:

1. The school minibus is involved in an accident while returning late at night from a school trip. Several pupils have minor injuries and are taken to hospital. The headteacher is woken by a local reporter asking for verification of the story.

2. A sudden spate of truancy amongst pupils in the school sparks an investigation by a local radio news reporter: how do you react without causing further problems among parents and staff?

3. The local paper offers last minute advertising space cheaply but with a tight deadline. Is it the right time and place to advertise? Who should make a decision? Are there suitable ads already available? If not, what will be the cost of creating one?

4. The open days are looming but the school prospectus isn't yet ready because further correections were needed at the last minute. The printer says it will cost extra and take more time. How could this have been avoided? Who should take responsibility for planning and production? And what should be done now to get around the problem?

As you read this book you will realise that marketing is not entirely a black art - much of it is common sense. You will find that many of your activities form a part of marketing, even if you don't think of them as such. I hope *Marketing your School* will give you more ideas and help you relate them to your existing activities in a plan that will prove effective for the future of your school.

Chapter 2
Know your
customers

One of the most important aspects of marketing is to establish clear customer benefits. But people are all different, and what one person sees as a benefit another may regard as a disadvantage. You need to understand why people choose to send their children to your school. Getting to know your customers is a necessary precursor to identifying benefits and using them as part of an effective marketing campaign.

Who are your customers?

Except for brand new schools which have not yet opened their doors, every school has an existing customer base - the parents of current pupils. The pupils themselves are consumers of the education the school provides. However, you should view them as customers too. As they grow up they will be more and more actively involved in the decision to stay at a school and in choosing their next school. Their progress and happiness at school are essential in creating customer satisfaction.

Satisfied customers help a school gain future customers since word of mouth is important in spreading a school's reputation, especially if it largely caters for a closely knit religious, ethnic or geographic community. Satisfied parents are more likely to send their other children to the school.

To determine who your potential customers are you need to know what sort of people choose to send their children to the school, in terms of socio-economic and geographic factors, and whether any changes are taking place which may affect your intake. By obtaining such information you can be proactive in adapting your school to future requirements. Consider the fictional situations outlined below and try answering those questions which apply to each scenario. You can then extend your thinking to the situation at your own school.

1. What social changes are taking place in the area which could affect the school's customer base?

2. Which groups of people should the school be communicating with?

3. What local problems will cause the school difficulty?

4. How can the school address any problems and needs that arise, given the nature of its main customer base?

5. What other types of customer does the school need to attend to ensure survival or expansion?

6. Where might the school find other customers?

7. What changes should it make to attract more customers?

8. What local circumstances can be used to the school's advantage?

9. How can the school differentiate itself from its competitors?

10. What should be the main objective of the school's marketing activities?

1. Greenfields Primary School
is in a rural village, a few miles from the local market town. The population of the village has declined to just a few hundred in recent years. Agricultural employment has been reduced consider-

ably. In Bishop Hartwell, an electronics parts factory has recently opened, offering low-wage, part-time jobs. Several villagers are now employed at the factory. The local church, a supporter of the school, has merged with neighbouring parishes.

The school has a roll of just over 200, and needs to attract more children from surrounding villages to prevent the threat of closure. Some villages are just half a mile away, but transport is a problem, and the PTA is exploring the idea of a community minibus to collect and drop children at each end of the school day. The staff consists of a headteacher, three classroom teachers and ancillary helpers, and dinner ladies etc. There is a threat that when the senior teacher retires at the end of the year, a replacement will be appointed at a lower level until the school roll increases. The local PTA is very supportive - several wealthy parents live in the area - and the school is well-resourced with books and computers, but lacks modern buildings. However Greenfields is surrounded by countryside, there is a stream running through the grounds and local woods provide splendid resources for natural history lessons.

2. St James Primary School
is in a medium sized town in a prosperous area. The school recently went grant-maintained, and prides itself on its record of excellence in curriculum attainment. Proximity to the nearby Army barracks creates special problems. Army children are frequently moved, so the school has to cope with children constantly joining and leaving, often at short notice of less than a term and sometimes just a week or two. The town is a centre for the computer industry, so there are a lot of well-paid, skilled jobs available, and firms are relocating to the area or starting up on the local industrial estate. This means that parents are usually employed, well paid, and can provide help with IT, especially with spare or old computers. St James has a large playground, and good buildings, but no playing field of its own. Children are taken to local community-owned facilities twice a week; and school trips are a regular feature. Parents are expected to contribute to these. The

teaching staff is good, with two students on teaching practice, although the high incidence of working mothers makes it hard to attract classroom helpers. The PTA supports the school with money for extra resources. It has not proved possible to fill the complement of parent Governors, now seen as an arduous, unfulfilling position with overwhelming responsibilities.

3. The Cllr. Rakih Singh School
is in a suburb of a large city in the eastern half of the country, mainly populated by immigrants from India, Africa and the Far East. Although the community is largely peaceful, there have been tensions recently, especially when there were riots at the local recently-privatised prison. The school, which has a roll of over 700, is highly regarded, can provide teaching in four languages, and sends several pupils each year to university and college. There are strong links with local FE colleges, and a special needs unit in the school attracts children from over twenty miles away. LEA budget cuts potentially mean losing three teachers at the end of the financial year. Because of the high cost of maintaining the old, rambling and inefficient buildings, resources are stretched to the limit with children using old computers and even older books. In spite of this, the community supports the school strongly and helps as much as it can. Some of the parents are professionals, but much of the local employment - often part-time - is in the local factories (cars, and aerospace).

4. The Smith-Walker Endowed School
opens in the autumn, on a newly-created housing estate of over 2,000 families in what was previously green belt land to the north west of London. At the moment, the area is a building site, with half-finished houses, flats, shops and roads; and the school is only three-quarters finished. If the school is successful, extra land has been acquired for Phase 2 which would start building next year. The Head, moved from another school nearby, has been in post since early in the year, and is recruiting staff ready for the school's opening in September. She is keen to set the school up as a dis-

tinctive cultural centre for the community from the start, and wants an open-school policy, with the school accessible fifteen hours a day for Open University courses, local groups and societies, and community involvement. The school opens in September with just 150 children, but will quickly reach 600+ by the year end. Local industry, keen to attract good quality employees to their kitchen unit and seismic instrumentation factories, are generous with their support for the school, both financial and material.

5. The Nigel Smithers Memorial School
is in a university town. The school was established just after the Second World War, and competes with a number of private schools in the town - a convent foundation, a small girls' school and a failing minor public school.

The Head of Nigel Smithers, which was formerly a grammar school, sees an opportunity to increase the school roll through acquisition of local day boys currently attending the independent school, and the threat of closure of a smaller school. The school site has room for another building, and the Head's ambition is to establish a sixth form, so that A level pupils would not have to travel ten miles to the local sixth form college. But several governors who are cautious about development and the PTA's aggressive fund-raising efforts have caused some rifts among certain groups of parents.

You may find it useful to come back to these examples and consider them against a wider range of marketing issues once you have finished reading this book.

Meanwhile, when considering your customer base, do not neglect former pupils: some may become future customers, if they continue to live in the area, or remain loyal to their *alma mater* in the independent sector. Certainly, independent schools see value in maintaining links with their former pupils. Most have some type of former students' society with regular gatherings, some annual information from the school and the prospect of this group helping to raise funds. Obviously, if former pupils have a negative view of the school, you will need to work extra hard to show how things have changed since then. You should also try to ensure that, even if the school has not met the needs of a particular individual, the parent and pupil think the right efforts were made and will not denigrate the school. The school must be seen in a positive light even though it may not be right for every individual.

Having determined who your current and likely future customers are, you are in a much better position to find out about their needs, and then to develop the school to meet those needs and so be seen to provide benefits. However, there is more to understanding customers than simply knowing who they are and what they want. It is also helpful to have some understanding about how they choose products, since this can influence how you market the school.

How customers choose

When choosing any product, customers behave in a variety of ways to reach their decision. Some may carry out an exhaustive investigation into all products of a similar type, comparing and contrasting a whole range of features before selecting the product which most closely matches their requirements. Theirs is an apparently rational approach. Others may base their decision on an overall emotional response, formed from first impressions, friends' recommendations and the general reputation of the available products. When choosing a school, people's behaviour is no different.

If customers are going to choose a product they must first be aware that it exists - hence the need for promotion. When buying a product like a soap powder, they may simply try it and then decide whether to buy it again. With major decisions such as choosing a car, a house or an education the process is more complex, and many other factors will influence their decision.

Economic considerations usually dictate whether or not people opt for independent education. For parents who decide this is not a possibility, social factors will come into play. For secondary schools, peer group pressure can be important in this respect, because most children want to attend the same school as their friends. Maintaining close links with feeder primary schools can therefore provide the impetus for children from those schools to choose your school. Some parents may have aspirations for their children to have a better start educationally than they had; and many of these believe that an independent school provides the answer, or a state school which has a similar ethos. If there is any indication that a large number of parents in your school's catchment area feel this way, your marketing could emphasise factors such as strong discipline which will influence their decision.

Even people who have adopted a very reasoned approach to choosing can be swayed by the most unlikely things. For example if they think you made an introductory speech on the open evening that was unnecessarily long or even boring, this single factor could outweigh many otherwise good impressions. They may think this is how their child will react in assembly or, even worse, during lessons. A chance comment from a student on open evening could influence their decision in either direction. You cannot control everything that everyone says about the school. Your main marketing concern should be to paint an accurate picture of the school, emphasising its positive attributes, so that customers do not feel let down by the reality when their child starts at the school.

Every school is different. Location, size and educational philosophy are just some of the factors which will affect the pupil intake and influence people's choice. Understanding customers' motivation is important and can help you develop effective marketing strategies for the future. If yours is a small village primary school with little local competition, your marketing requirements will be very different from those of a large independent boarding school which seeks to attract pupils from affluent families across the country and maybe the world. But if your village school is in an affluent area you may still lose some of your pupils to an independent school midway through their primary school career. The number lost will be lower if you are providing good customer satisfaction - ie. the type of education parents in your area want for their children.

Why people choose your school

You may be aware of the main reasons why parents choose your school but nevertheless be surprised by others. A particular feature which you might not have seen as a significant benefit may be important to a considerable number of existing parents and therefore should be included in your marketing plans. Alternatively you may find that most parents feel they have little choice but to send their children to the school but do not perceive any specific benefits. If this is the case you will have to work hard to attract future pupils to the school.

Find out the main reasons why parents feel constrained to send their children to the school. Proximity may be one. This could be seen as a benefit, but is only likely to be viewed in a positive light if there are other benefits. So you will need to find out what a majority of local parents want from the school and focus on achieving their main priorities. If they see the school is changing to meet their needs they will begin to recognise that it is benefiting their children.

Consider the many factors which influence people's choice of a school: location, size, uniform policy, single sex or co-educational, atmosphere, academic reputation, position in the school league tables compared with competing schools, reputation as a centre of excellence in one or more subjects, reputation for providing a good all round education, discipline, social ethos, the school environment - building and grounds, sporting reputation, range of subjects taught, extra curricular provision, special needs provision and so on. The list is extensive, but they will all feature to a greater or lesser extent in people's reasons for choosing the school and you need to know which matter most to the people in your intake area.

In total, the particular features which combine to give your school its character, amount to a product. Chapter 3 discusses the school as a product to be marketed. Then, in chapter 4, we will look at market research - the means of obtaining information to support your marketing activities.

Chapter 3
The school as
a product

Most parents have definite views about the type of education they want for their child. Whether this is based on their own aspirations, a reaction in favour of or against the education they themselves received, knowledge of their children's interests and abilities, or a combination of these factors, they will be looking for a school that offers a particular type of education.

In selecting an education for their children they will consider not just what is taught but the whole ethos of the school - its buildings and grounds, culture and style, extra-curricular activities and facilities, the quality of its teachers and management, the options offered, its size and a host of other factors. From a parent's point of view, the school is a product.

Choices available in education

The amount of choice people have when seeking a school for their child varies with their economic circumstances and where they live. Different types of educational institution cater for various stages in a child's development. As yet, not everyone using the state education system is fortunate enough to have a local nursery school and in some rural areas the choice of primary school may be restricted, but by the time children reach secondary level most people can choose from a range of different establishments: county schools, voluntary aided and voluntary controlled, grant maintained and special maintained schools, further education and sixth form colleges. Some schools have religious affiliations, some are single sex schools, some are comprehensive in their intake while others have a selective admission policy.

Usually one or two key factors determine which schools people decide to visit for a more detailed assessment. For some, religious affiliation will be the top priority with academic excellence next; others may want a single sex school which is non-selective and has good sports facilities; another group may opt for academic excellence and selective admission but be less concerned whether the school is co-ed or single sex; others may place emphasis on the school's reputation for music or art. If your school does not fit their initial criteria, parents are unlikely to consider it.

Key factors which influence choice of school

	Yes	No
religious affiliation		
academic excellence		
all round education		
single sex		
extra-curricular provision		
reputation for music		
reputation for art		
reputation for good maths teaching		
wide range of sports offered		
good playing fields		
class size		
uniform		
discipline		

However even when your school matches parents' initial requirements you cannot afford to be complacent. There may well be several others which provide an equally good match. In city areas there may be a number of similar primary schools within relatively easy reach of many pupils and in most localities there is a choice of two or three comprehensive or other secondary schools accessible by public transport or school bus.

Product differentiation

The marketing challenge is to differentiate your school from the others so that parents will single it out as having that extra something they are looking for. You have to convince them that your school is preferable to the competition. To be convincing you need to be confident about what you are offering. If the product is not up to standard it will need to be improved.

No school can be all things to all people so you have to decide what type of product you are offering. You also need to discover what your competitors are offering. Only then can you see where you offer a particular benefit that is not available elsewhere, but which could make a difference. Of course you may find that your competitors have features which differentiate them. You may decide to emulate some of the things they are doing or you may prefer, based on research of what customers want, to offer other alternatives. But you need to be alert to such differences and recognise their value in your marketing activities.

In some schools it may be obvious from falling numbers that the school is not doing as well as it should and that improvements must be made. Even if your school is doing well, you need to maintain its position. A thorough assessment of what the school offers compared to its competitors and what parents want is a useful exercise for ensuring that the most effective steps are taken to maintain or improve its performance and market it well.

The quality of educational provision may be the primary concern of most parents choosing a school but, no matter how good the educational standard, they are not going to be satisfied if they find the school is badly managed, budgets are poorly spent and class rooms are in poor repair. Just as companies can themselves be products to the share buying public who evaluate their performance and management as factors influencing their purchasing decision, so too a school in its entirety can be viewed as a product. In effect a detailed evaluation of the school is a product audit.

The product audit

Companies selling a range of products use product audits to assess the performance of each product and decide whether to discontinue some and introduce new ones. The school can only become a new product by changing its whole ethos. The need for such a fundamental change is usually easy to see but less obvious weaknesses may escape notice during the everyday running of the school and only be revealed by an audit.

The aim of the audit is to gather detailed information in a systematic way to give a comprehensive view of the school's position compared to its competitors within its segment of the education market. This information can then be analysed and used when making decisions about future marketing activities. Information about any areas of performance which may influence people's choice of the school should be an integral part of the audit.

Indeed an audit should review performance in all functions, including marketing. It should look at the overall marketing environment, assess the school's marketing activities and the systems it has to support these activities. In practice, of course, you can only do what is possible within your resources.

The information you will need about the marketing environment includes the size of the market and trends which may affect it (eg. the area has started to attract retired people so numbers of children of school age are diminishing); full details about the education the school offers (the product), and about all the school's competitors, their educational offering, reputation, marketing methods and any other information about them which could affect your school's performance and strategy.

Details about the school's marketing activities would include:
• a review of its marketing procedures and how its marketing is organised,
• information about what market research it undertakes
• factual and qualitative review of the school as a product, looking at all aspects of the school, including teaching and management capability, range of subjects and extra-curricular activities offered and planned (in other words detail from the product audit)
• promotional activities: public relations, advertising, publications, events
• provision of customer service and benefits.

An audit of the school's marketing systems should reveal
• what the school's marketing objectives are
• whether it has a marketing strategy to achieve those objectives, plus plans based on that strategy and adequate resources, including well defined responsibilities
• whether effective systems are in place for obtaining marketing information and making it accessible to people making marketing decisions
• whether people with marketing responsibility have the authority to influence school policies

- whether there is sufficient measurement of the school's marketing activities to determine if they are meeting objectives cost-effectively.

Having gathered a large amount of information, you should analyse it in a way that will support the decision making needed for developing marketing plans. This is best done by performing a SWOT analysis.

SWOT analysis...

...is so called because information is categorised under four headings: strengths, weaknesses, opportunities and threats. By selecting key items of information from the audit and presenting it in this way you reduce a large volume of data to manageable proportions and can recognise the strengths and weaknesses of the school compared to its competitors, see where any opportunities exist and identify any threats to the school's continued success or survival, either from competitors or external circumstances. It then becomes clear where action is needed for improvements and what items can be harnessed for marketing purposes.

It would probably be over ambitious to suggest that schools carry out a full audit every year though this should not become an excuse for never doing one. It is worth performing a SWOT analysis annually. By doing so you will be forced to look critically at the school, notice changes and to some extent update the previous audit. These activities should be the starting point for developing the school's marketing plan each year.

Opposite is an example of a SWOT analysis for a fictional primary school:

Using this example as a starting point, you should be able to construct a SWOT analysis for your school. You may need to discuss the strengths, weaknesses, opportunities and threats with your colleagues - and you will need some detachment.

Strengths	Weaknesses
• maths teaching now excellent • closer to good public transport and safe cycle route than nearby state primaries • one staff member is an art and design specialist	• the music teacher has left and there is no teacher able to continue school's music at previous level
Opportunities	Threats
• start a maths club • also an art club (but art teacher has to leave by 4.30 each day) • supportive PTA	• nearby private school offers good music tuition and wide range of extra curricular activities • nearest state primary offers football after school once a week and may extend this to after school care every day

Who should conduct an audit?

You could commission a management or marketing consultant to undertake an audit, defining the functions to be considered if you can undertake some yourself. This may be worthwhile as a basis for the future, since it could provide a framework to follow and update for some years to come. You may find that the report by the school inspectorate provides a useful basis for a marketing audit if you add some additional information. You may also be able to draw on the expertise of school parents and governors with marketing experience. Even if they cannot carry out the entire exercise they may be able to advise the school and provide the basic structure and system for those responsible for marketing to use.

So far you have seen the need to amass a great deal of information about the school, its competitors and customers. How to obtain this information is the subject of the next chapter.

Chapter 4
Market research

The term 'market research' conjures up the image of a person with a clipboard in the local shopping centre who stops passers-by to ask their views on all sorts of subjects and ticks their answers to multi-choice questions on a carefully arranged form. Such surveys are one way of obtaining information. However they are not the only way, and they are the least likely to be used by a school - though some people may be only too willing to give their opinion if, for example, they think all the pupils are thoroughly unruly and badly behaved on the bus each day.

Instead you need to undertake market research which is structured to meet your specific objectives. Market research is the process of assembling relevant data, analysing and presenting it in a way that will support decision making for marketing purposes.

You have already seen the need to gather information about customers, potential customers, their levels of satisfaction, about competitors and about the school itself. Obviously much of this information is already available within the school. However it is probably widely dispersed, some being known only to individual teachers and administrative staff. Therefore a system is needed to assemble relevant information so that it becomes accessible for marketing purposes. Avoid collecting non-essential information which may be interesting but will simply prove distracting and make data analysis more difficult.

Be clear about your goals

Most schools are hard pressed to allocate resources for non-classroom activities, so be clear about your goals before you start. What do you want to achieve from this piece of market research? Who will analyse the data? How will you use it?

Start by listing all the items of information you need and beside each item note possible sources for obtaining the information. The table on p. 28 shows a simplified version of what such a list might look like.

If information is available from members of staff or from articles in newspapers and similar sources, you will need to establish a suitable system for collecting and filing it or it will not be available when needed. Prioritise the information you need from staff so that they are not over-burdened and you can eliminate the lower priority items if resources are limited. If particular teachers regularly hold joint activities with other schools you should ask them to provide feedback about significant information they obtain during their visits. Similarly staff attending conferences or courses can provide feedback about competitors, or suggestions about what other schools are doing which could be introduced to improve your school.

Some staff may take the initiative and provide the information but in general teachers are so busy that unless they have been alerted to the need and a formal feedback procedure has been established the information will not be forthcoming. A feedback form - keep it as short as reasonably possible to encourage responses - should be introduced with an explanation about why the information is necessary. Then staff will be less likely to see the form as

Information required and likely sources

Information needed	Primary data source	Other sources
Customers		
proportion of girls/boys	school roll	
proportion of non-English speakers	school roll	
proportion taking free school meals	school roll	
proportion of each ethnic group	school roll	
proportion of difficult students in each class	class/subject teacher	
benefits sought	parental survey	
customer satisfaction rating	parental survey	
demographic trends which will affect intake	LEA / Local Chamber of Commerce	
Competitors		
School A	sports teacher	teacher going to a conference, LEA, School league tables, local media, school prospectus
School B	drama teacher	LEA, School league tables, local media, school prospectus
Your school		
Quality of individual teaching in various subjects	Head of subject	Deputy heads, head of year groups, OFSTED report, exam results, letters/comments from parents
Truancy	Form teachers	
Management	OFSTED report	

an unnecessary piece of bureaucracy and, at the same time, their awareness of why and how the school must market itself will increase. If they are also aware that you don't expect information from every outside event, especially if they regularly visit another school, they won't grasp at straws and provide information that is only marginally useful. Reasonably frequent reminders at staff meetings of the need for information, identifying areas that are of current concern, should ensure suitable input. The same form could also be used for staff to contribute information gained at other times, for example when parents and others attend events at the school or ask to meet them to discuss children's progress. It would need to be structured in a manner that would elicit relevant information to meet the school's marketing objectives.

Where there are gaps among your sources of information you will have to decide how important the information is, how to obtain it and which areas have priority.

```
Memo to all staff
Subject: introduction of feedback form

We need to ensure that Wellborough High School con-
tinues to provide a well rounded education for its
students that satisfies parents' expectations and
compares well with its competitors. We can only do so
if we understand parents' requirements of the school
and know as much as possible about our competitors'
offerings. When you attend outside events, such as
conferences or interschool activities, or meet par-
ents individually or at parents' evenings you may
obtain information that will be useful in planning
the school's future. So that this information is not
lost or forgotten please fill in the attached feed-
back form and return it to the school office so that
```

Wellborough High School - Feedback form

NAME: .... DATE: / / ....

EVENT ATTENDED: ....

Information about Wellborough Comprehensive
Nature of information: please tick appropriate item(s) and column
praise   complaint
          Facilities
          Teaching
          Truancy rates
          Bullying
          Sports
          extracurricular provision
          special needs provision
          English as a second language teaching
          other

Please explain in more detail:
....

Information about a competitor
Nature of information:
praise   complaint
          Facilities
          Teaching
          Truancy rates
          Bullying
          Sports
          extracurricular provision
          innovation in any area
          other

Please explain in more detail:
....
Any other comments:
....

An alternative feedback form could be devised which would require respondents to evaluate the information obtained on a scale from poor to excellent as in the following example:

Wellborough High School - Feedback form

NAME: DATE: /   /

EVENT ATTENDED:

Information obtained from:
Information about Wellborough Comprehensive
Circle the box which most closely matches the information obtained
1= excellent 2= good 3= satisfactory 4= unsatisfactory 5= poor

Library	1	2	3	4	5
Text book provision	1	2	3	4	5
Facilities	1	2	3	4	5

State which facilities the answer above refers to

Teaching:	1	2	3	4	5

State which subject(s) the answer above refers to

Sports	1	2	3	4	5

State which sport(s) the answer above refers to

extracurricular	1	2	3	4	5
special needs	1	2	3	4	5
ESL teaching	1	2	3	4	5
other	1	2	3	4	5

For the items below 1= none 2= very little 3= average 4= above average 5= very high level

Truancy rates	1	2	3	4	5
Bullying	1	2	3	4	5

Please add any relevant details

If you wish to obtain views about a particular item you may need to devise a questionnaire specifically for that purpose. For example if your school has raised a large sum of money and needs to decide which among a number of items it should be spent on you may wish to ask parents their views. There are a number of ways in which the same question can be asked. Three possibilities are shown: the first invites an unlimited range of views, being a completely open question; the second limits the options; the third focuses on one item but also provides a means of estimating what would be most favoured if the chosen option proves unpopular.

1. How would you like the funds to be spent?

....

2. Would you like the funds to be spent on
   A: Books B: Sports equipment C: New minibus
   D: Trees and grassed area in the playground?

3. Would you like the school to buy a new minibus?

   Yes   No   Don't know

If you have answered 'No', which alternative would you prefer?

   a) books

   b) sports equipment

   c) trees and a grassed area in the playground

How to obtain information

You can use a number of methods to obtain information that is not readily available. You could bring in a marketing consultant to carry out a survey. You could use internal resources to conduct a survey yourself. You could canvass opinion at school events. Consider inexpensive methods of obtaining the information, such as carrying out a survey yourself.

If the school has adequate funds, paying an external consultant to undertake a specific project may be the most appropriate course, particularly if the survey to be undertaken is complex and requires substantial data analysis by computer. An outside consultant could also be commissioned to provide the school with suitable systems for future internal use. Obtain several quotes, if possible from firms which have been recommended and understand the issues facing schools, and ask to see samples of their work, just as you would when hiring any other contractor. To get maximum value from using an outside consultant you need to be very thorough in preparing the brief and know the limits of what you want done. If you leave it to the consultant to come up with suggestions about what is needed costs could escalate - though you don't have to accept all the suggestions.

Before employing an outside consultant you should consider whether any of the tasks can be done internally. You may have a school governor with business experience who can advise on the best approach to a specific project. Many schools have willing parents who come to parent/teacher evenings because they want to help the school. Often they help by raising funds for the school but there is no reason why they should not help in other ways. So ask if there are any parents with enough knowledge of marketing, market research and similar areas of business to join a working party for the projects you have in mind.

If the research is fairly straightforward staff could handle some projects themselves but when weighing up the costs of doing something internally against employing a consultant you need a realistic estimate of how much staff time it will take and their ability to complete the job.

Both interviews and questionnaires can be used to obtain information. In either case you need to formulate the questions carefully. Open questions such as 'What aspects of the school's performance could be improved?' will produce widely varying responses which can make data analysis more difficult 37than closed questions such as 'Are you satisfied with the standard of science teaching?' which elicit a simple 'yes' or 'no' or 'don't know' answer and can easily be counted to discover the overall level of satisfaction.

In questionnaires you can use slightly more sophisticated methods, asking respondents to rank their views on a scale of 1 - 5. (Make sure you specify that 1 = excellent / very satisfied / very important, down to 5 = poor / not satisfied / unimportant, or vice versa.) The answers can be given weightings and counted to gain more detail about people's views than is possible with a simple yes/no response. For example to discover more about why parents choose the school you could ask them to complete a questionnaire when their child enters the school which includes questions such as:

Which of the following factors was important to you in choosing to send your child to the school? (1= very important, 2= important, 3= quite important, 4= less important, 5= unimportant.)

academic reputation	1	2	3	4	5
good public transport	1	2	3	4	5
school uniform	1	2	3	4	5
single sex	1	2	3	4	5
religious affiliation	1	2	3	4	5
sports offered	1	2	3	4	5
extra curricular activities	1	2	3	4	5
reputation for music	1	2	3	4	5
reputation for art	1	2	3	4	5
special needs provision	1	2	3	4	5

You could add a final open question asking respondents to state any other reasons which have not been listed in order to identify reasons that you may not previously have considered. The questions you decide to ask will depend on what your objectives are. If you are interested in discovering how much influence your marketing has had on people's choice you could include a question asking about factors such as the impression created on open day, information from the school prospectus, the reputation of the school and so forth. You might then go on to establish how they had gained their knowledge of the school's reputation, listing possibilities such as word of mouth and newspaper articles.

Some research must be conducted by the school itself. For example you should seek feedback on why pupils leave to go to another school, both midway through their school career and at the major times of change such as after their GCSEs. A pattern may emerge from such information that shows a weakness that could be remedied.

It is also possible that some small area of research could form part of a geography, sociology or business studies assignment which secondary students could undertake. You may obtain local demographic information in this way or assess the affect that the building of a new housing development may have on the local area. The teacher supervising such projects could extract some of the information for marketing purposes.

Various events held at the school, such as parent/teacher meetings, open days, school fairs and other fund raising occasions, also provide an opportunity to obtain information from parents, prospective parents and the local community. A simple show of hands at parents' meetings or open days for prospective parents may give an indication of how people view certain proposals or services. For example some existing parents may have expressed a need for after school child care. If you are debating whether this could be provided on the school premises and whether it would influence more people to send their children to the school, an idea of how many people might be interested could be obtained by this simple expedient. If the response indicated sufficient interest, it would then be worthwhile to investigate possible ways of establishing a service, looking at legal and insurance requirements before conducting a more comprehensive survey to ensure the proposed scheme would be acceptable. Of course research might reveal that just such a scheme was about to be started at another nearby school. Knowing this in advance could save your school taking the wrong action. After all, research is simply a tool to aid decision making.

You may be able to canvas the views of members of your local community by linking a brief questionnaire to a prize draw at a school event, such as a school fair or jumble sale. However the value of such information would be limited if the sample providing answers was heavily biased toward one group in the community. For example, if there were a large number of people in the school's catchment area whose mother tongue is not English, many of them would have difficulty completing a questionnaire so other methods of obtaining their views would have to be found.

Quality of information

The quality of the information obtained from interviews, questionnaires and other forms of feedback will vary depending on the style and scale of market research, the timeliness of the information and how credible the information source is. The person responsible for marketing should develop a critical attitude and an awareness of possible weaknesses in the information from particular sources. Feedback about the same subject from a second source can help dispel or confirm doubts about the accuracy of the information and indicate how much reliance to place on it when making decisions.

The more comprehensive the survey is, the more likely it is that the results will be helpful. However it is not necessary to obtain the views of every person in a group. A representative sample of views can be taken by including the correct proportion of each ethnic minority, sex and social class and other sub-group so the sample reflects the profile of the entire group. By taking a sample of views you reduce the volume of data you have to analyse. This is helpful if resources are limited.

Data analysis

Market research involves not just information gathering but also analysing and interpreting the information so that it can be used as a basis for making marketing decisions.

If yours is a large secondary school that needs to collect and analyse a large amount of data you could discuss what is required with information technology and business studies staff. They may be able to help in some areas. If the school is smaller the volume of data will be less daunting so it should be possible to sort the data into suitable categories to support decision making. Quantitative data - answers which can be counted - are easier to organise than qualitative, which require some subjective judgements to be made. Common patterns should become apparent if the information is well organised. However if complex research has been undertaken or if the outcome of a decision based on the research will have far reaching consequences it would be advisable to call in an expert to help organise information and interpret the results.

Chapter 5
Public relations

The essence of promotion is communication. In this book the concept of promoting a school is taken in its widest sense to cover public relations, marketing literature and advertising. This chapter deals with public relations and later chapters will look at other areas.

Public relations, often abbreviated to PR, comprises activities designed to foster and maintain a good relationship between an organisation and its different publics. The practice is particularly concerned with promulgating positive messages that will influence selected audiences to form a favourable image of the organisation.

Image

Each person's image of the school will differ slightly depending on their individual prejudices and their experience of the school. For some outsiders a smart school uniform will earn the school a good reputation, whereas others will regard a playground full of happily occupied students as a better indication of the quality of a school.

A school's image is made up of a whole variety of things from the overall appearance of the school buildings to the behaviour of the students. Aspects of the school's physical appearance which contribute to its image are:

School uniform

Each school must decide its own policy about uniform and some may decide against having one. Prevailing teenage fashions militate against a smart appearance among many secondary school pupils even when they are in uniform.

School badge or logo

A school badge or logo appearing on school uniforms, correspondence, school vehicles, and notice boards and signs around the school give the school an identity and encourage a feeling of belonging and a sense of pride among staff and students - provided there is a solid foundation for such feelings. Some schools may have a motto. If it is meaningful to the pupils it can reinforce the effect of the logo.

School badges can convey different messages as instanced by these from Holy Rood School, Edinburgh and Milford School, Devon

Signs

Signs should be well painted and prominently displayed, with clear permanent pointers to reception and other areas used regularly by visitors and temporary directions to other areas for occasional events such as parents' evenings. Good clear signage is an addition to security within school.

Buildings

Buildings should be well maintained and painted. In many people's eyes signs of physical neglect, such as peeling paint, go hand in hand with poorly motivated staff and pupils and therefore tarnish the school's reputation. The toilets should be kept clean and efforts should be made to counteract the drab uniformity of long corridors by displays of students' work. At the very least they should be clear and brightly lit. Classrooms should show signs of interesting educational activities - this is usually well managed in primary schools where children's work is frequently displayed but similar recognition given to work done in secondary schools can also enhance the school's image and boost student morale.

Reception

The reception area should be constantly attended or at least have a bell which will be promptly answered; there should be a welcoming atmosphere, seats, some up-to-date school literature in pristine condition for the visitor to read, possibly some paintings on the walls, and student work or framed awards on display to add interest and make the most of every opportunity to show the school's achievements to best advantage. The reception area is also a focus for security - ensuring visitors have badges and are logged in and out, for example.

School grounds

The grounds should be tidy and if possible made more inviting with trees, plants and flowers. Untidy school grounds convey the impression that the school does not value itself highly and therefore will not value its students. Like the staff, they will be happier and better motivated in pleasant surroundings. Ensure that there are enough litter and recycling bins throughout the school and involve pupils in an environmental awareness or recycling campaign to gain some enthusiasm for putting papers, bottles and cans in the correct bins and keeping them off the ground.

External communications

External communications, from press releases, advertisements and marketing literature to regular correspondence with parents, should be designed to enhance the school's image, as described in coming sections.

Other factors which contribute to the school's image are:

The telephone

Some people may gain their first impression of the school by telephone. They may have obtained the name of the school from the local education authority because they are about to move to the area. All will be well if they receive a friendly response from the person answering the phone and their query is dealt with efficiently. However if the phone is not answered for ages or the person who answers it is very abrupt - perhaps for understandable reasons - it will nevertheless leave the caller with a dissatisfied feeling about the school.

Staff motivation

Well motivated staff play a huge part in building and maintaining the school's reputation - but this is the domain of professional educationalists.

Student behaviour

The behaviour of students can make or break a school's reputation. Children who bump into passers by as they rush out of school will dispel a previously favourable perception created by a smart uniform. However pupils who return a lost handbag with the contents intact will gain credit for the school, and if the owner writes to commend the school about the honesty of its pupils, the fact can be widely communicated at the school assembly and through the school newsletter or bulletin to parents. These actions cannot be dictated but the attitudes engendered within the school help determine the type of behaviour that is most likely to occur outside its gates. Again behaviour and discipline are best left to teachers.

Events

How well the school organises and presents itself at events influences people's views about the school. (See chapter 9.)

All these elements combine to create the public perception of the school. Like it or not, external appearances play a considerable part in building a school's image. The public school tradition in British education is linked by many with academic excellence so some schools wanting such a reputation may choose to emulate the popular perception of the public school by deliberately emphasising such elements as smart school uniform, an attractive environment and well presented publications.

However if the perception does not match the reality you can be sure people will find out, though a decline will be more rapidly noticed than an improvement. It takes no time at all for news to spread if standards fall or there is a drugs scandal at a school which has previously had a good reputation. On the other hand, if a school has improved you will have to work particularly hard at promotional activities to communicate the changes and it will take time for earlier negative views to be corrected.

Mission statements

Businesses in the nineties often have a mission statement. By declaring their mission - their rationale for being in business - and promulgating the statement throughout the company they expect staff to understand and work to achieve their mission. Such statements must be succinct and memorable if they are to be effective.

Some schools have also decided to create mission statements. Others may regard such a statement as too formal for their environment. Nevertheless the exercise of considering what the school's purpose is and encapsulating it in a brief statement can be useful. It forces you to focus on exactly what type of educational institution your school is and what you want it to achieve. By ensuring that staff and students know and understand this, everyone can work together, sharing the same underlying values and goals. Together with the school identity this helps foster loyalty.

Here are two mission statements, taken from the schools' prospectuses:

We learn to live in a changing world

To achieve this we do the following:

Learning
- we encourage students to enjoy the challenge of learning
- we expect high standards of achievement
- we seek to enable all individuals to fulfil their potential

Living
- we work together in a positive, open atmosphere
- we share a rich and dynamic, international community full of life, energy and creativity
- we expect behaviour which demonstrates care and concern for others

People for a changing world
- we develop self confidence, kindness, courage and the capacity to be critical
- we prepare young people for the future as active and flexible contributors to a demanding world in the new information age

HOLLAND PARK SCHOOL, LONDON W11

> To promote a learning environment in which all within the school community feel valued, supported and able to realise their full potential, thus ensuring that Wilmslow High is a school of first choice.
>
> WILMSLOW HIGH SCHOOL, WILMSLOW, CHESHIRE

Public relations programme

There are many ways in which you can influence people's view of the school for which you are responsible. Depending on your aims and budget, your school may select a variety of elements to make up its public relations programme, including:

- Customer relations
- Community relations
- Media relations
- Crisis management
- Sponsorship (see chapter 6, page 67).

In undertaking any of these activities it is important to be sure of your objectives, be aware of what will attract and interest your target audience and what messages you wish to convey to each audience to achieve your objective. If your school is in a disadvantaged area you may have an uphill struggle to persuade people to send their children there rather than to a school a few miles away in a more prosperous area. You may need to educate parents and the local population that not all schools can be top of the league table; that the figures should be taken in context with social and economic factors; that schools which do not select their intake according to academic merit can be successful if they help all their students fulfil their potential and gain confidence as human beings. Your objective at a school open day would be to change attitudes, your audience would be parents and prospective parents in your area and the message would be that league tables are not all-important; there are many other criteria for judging the success of a non-selective school, and then focus on your school's strengths.

Customers

A main audience for any school is its parent body - the school's customers. Communications with parents should be planned if they are to be effective. Primary schools have an advantage, as children are usually collected from school by an adult who may be a parent or else can pass any communication to the parent. Secondary schools cannot be sure that information sent home by pupil post will be given to the parents.

The dates of many key events in the school year can be planned well ahead and notified to parents in a letter posted at the start of the school year. If the school has an itinerant population it may be difficult to reach every parent, but the same letter should be provided as new pupils enrol during the year. In this letter you can explain homework policy and how parents can obtain information about it, and school policies about uniform, behaviour and discipline. Avoid burdening parents with too much information in one communication, otherwise the item you consider most important may not gain their attention. Clear presentation of the information will help.

You also need to reach the parents of the students of the future. Here you need to cast your net wider. Primary schools can develop contacts with local playgroups, nurseries, child minders, churches, libraries etc. - anywhere that parents may take children. If there is a toddlers' club in the local park, that's where the school's information or name should be known. If you are able to take children from a considerable distance away you need to consider sending information to all relevant libraries, and to churches if yours is a church school. A similar range of options should be pursued at secondary level: links with the primary schools from which they draw their intake will replace playgroups and nurseries.

Word of mouth communication within the local area and among the school community is a powerful force. The school gate of pri-

THE SUMMER FAIR

HEY, DON'T FORGET TO TAKE ME HOME!

THE BIGGEST *FUN*DRAISER OF THE YEAR

Dear Parent / Guardian,

On June 6 we will be holding our Summer fair - the biggest fundraiser of the year.

In order for us to buy resources, sports equipment, books, IT equipment

WE NEED

Helpers, Cooks, Bric-à-brac, Bottles - and a huge attendance!

FOR our Tombola, Lucky dip, Lotto, Coconut shy, Treasure Hunt, Donkey Rides, Bouncy Castle, White Elephant Stall

On June 6th, 2.00, at: Stythy House Primary School, Horseradish Lane, Finchingham.

- -

REPLY FORM

YES - I CAN HELP

Name:

Telephone:

Volunteering for:

Please return this form to your class teacher

When you have to rely on pupil post a letter like this reminds the messenger to deliver it, and stands a chance of getting home.

mary schools is an important meeting point for local parents where they glean all sorts of information and impressions about local schools, both other primary schools in the area and the secondary schools to which their children may progress. Some of these parents may have children who are already at secondary school. By maintaining good relationships with their parents, secondary schools can create ambassadors who spread the work about them in their catchment area.

The Local Community

The school is part of a local community and should therefore try to develop and maintain a good reputation within the area. If your school is proactive in developing links with other local institutions, they will gain an understanding of the school's aspirations, of any difficulties it may face and how it is working to overcome them. This could lead to some joint initiatives which will help the school achieve some of its goals and enhance its reputation in the process.

The spin-off effects may be considerable. For example good relationships with local businesses may encourage them to take pupils for work experience or to sponsor a school activity (see the section on sponsorship in chapter 6). By developing contacts with other schools offering the same stage of education, you may be able to provide a wider scope of options through some joint activities. Such contacts can also help you remain aware of developments by competitors that could present a threat.

You should ensure that your school communicates well with feeder schools, from which you expect to draw future students. By providing these schools with up-to-date information about your school's activities, they become a channel through which you can reach your future customers.

The Media

The media are not a direct audience but they are a means by which you can influence public perception about your school. You

⊐ **Mickle Trafford Primary School** ···

TREE-MENDOUS EFFORT:

Ex-pupils of Mickle Trafford Primary School raised £96 which was used to buy a maple tree.

Thirty boys and girls baked cakes and made biscuits and sold them to the rest of the school during play times.

The former pupils, all now aged 12 and from Mickle Trafford, seen here helping to plant the tree, are Richard Knight, Katharine Moulton and Emma Aspinell.

With them is Sarah Scargill from the British Trust for Conservation Volunteers who holds the tree upright while current pupils and part time teacher Pip Greatorex give their support.
162884A

An example of a caption story

should use as many opportunities as possible to ensure that positive messages about the school are conveyed through your local media - TV, radio or newspapers. You do not want your first contact with the local press to be when the school chemistry lab catches fire. So part of your marketing plan should be to find or create some positive stories that will raise awareness about the school among the people you wish to influence, in particular the parents of current and future pupils.

Media relations policy

You need to do all you can to control communications flowing from the school to the outside world, and in particular to journalists. Therefore before you embark on a media relations campaign define a policy about who is authorised to speak to the press as an official representative of the school. Make sure that everyone is aware of the policy so that other members of staff and students understand that they are not authorised to speak for the school. If the governors appoint their own representative you should liaise closely with them to ensure that any statements they make are consistent with those of the school.

One person should be given responsibility for dealing with the press and be known as the main point of contact for journalists approaching the school for information. This could be the head teacher but may be someone else in a responsible position who will know when to deal with the query themselves and when to refer it to the head. The same person could be responsible for initiating press releases. If other demands on people's time mean that the responsibilities have to be divided there will need to be close co-ordination between all parties involved in issuing releases and making statements to the press, and this also takes time.

The person who initiates releases could call on willing and able parents to help draft press releases but ultimately the school should have ultimate editorial control. Of course, once a press release has been issued it is up to media editors to decide how they will use it and to edit it to suit their needs. By following the guidelines about writing releases on the next pages you should be able to reduce the amount of editing that will be needed and the chance of inaccuracies creeping in.

Get to know the local press. Look at the local papers to determine what type of story interests each one, whether there are any regular sections on education, young people, diary columns etc. Then create some stories to suit. You may send a press release with your own pictures to give the news or you may decide to invite local journalists or the local paper's photographer to report and photograph an event.

Do the local papers use many pictures? If not, why not? Perhaps you could send some different photos with a caption story. If you ask you may well find some enthusiastic amateur photographers among your parent body, who would be willing to take any photos you need. Obviously you would need to be satisfied that the photos had sufficient visual interest for the press to use - beware the tree accidentally growing out of someone's head and similar misfortunes that are not always noticed through the viewfinder. Provide a roll of film and the cost of processing to see what results can be achieved. Urge the photographer to take a good many shots from different angles so that a suitable photo emerges. The installation of new playground equipment or the opening of a new sports hall are obvious choices for some activity photos, but these events don't occur often. The retirement of the local lollipop lady or a local school bus driver after a long period serving the community - photographed with smiling children in readily identifiable uniforms - provide other examples of possible photo story opportunities. You must be sure the composition of the photos is interesting and the film quality is good enough for printing: ask the picture editor on the local paper you think has the best pictures what is needed for a photo to be accepted, or consult an experienced professional photographer.

Be careful not to publicise the activities of individual children without their full co-operation and their parents' agreement or you may be deemed to be exploiting them. This applies to other promotional activities too.

Think of every unique, unusual, first, new or best thing that has happened to anyone in the school when trying to find stories. In primary schools some examples could be a student growing the prize marrow at the local horticultural show, the school keeping an unusual pet; or progress reports about an injured animal that has been adopted by the school. You may find that among the five year olds starting school there are six boys called Tom. Instead of five guys named Moe you could provide a photo story to the local paper about six lads named Tom. With their agreement take a good photo of all six boys looking eager and alert, raising their hand when the teacher calls their name.

Different examples will be needed for secondary schools: does the school have an anniversary to celebrate? Have some students won an award? Is one of your sports teams doing particularly well? Has the school choir just made a recording? If your school wants to be seen as a centre of excellence for music, publicising the recording will help toward that objective.

If you can create stories about the school in association with other organisations which have their own public relations function you may be able to avoid writing some press releases and have a professional job done for you. If the school is named you should ask to see the release before it is issued in time to change sections of the text relating to the school, should it be necessary. In practice you may have to make comments within a 24 hour period.

Remember that journalists are busy people with deadlines to meet and plenty of other stories jostling for space in their editorial programme. So you need to be sure your press release gains their attention.

Here are some rules to follow which will help improve the quality of your press releases:
• Give your release a good headline
• Put the date on the release (you may have written it in advance but the date should be when you intend to send it, as close to the time of the news as possible while ensuring you meet editorial deadlines)
• Make your first paragraph tell the essential points of the story and then expand the story in subsequent paragraphs
• Keep the release short - two pages of A4 maximum
• Use short sentences and use active not passive verbs
• Use double spaced typing to allow the journalist to edit it
• Use an easy-to-read type size - such as 12 point

- Always use school letterhead with the words PRESS RELEASE or some variation (NEWS RELEASE, MEDIA INFORMATION etc.) in large bold print at the top or, if you have desktop publishing facilities, down the side (though this uses more space which you may wish to conserve for the story). You can set up suitable stationery templates in most word-processing programs. Creating printed letterhead purely for press releases is a more expensive idea.

- Ensure that contact details for further information are provided at the bottom - the minimum should be a name and telephone number.

- Having once decided on a suitable type style and letterhead for press releases keep using it - the consistent appearance will become part of the school's image in the eyes of the press.

- Send photos with a separate caption: an A4 sheet with explanatory text plus contact details, should be glued to the back of the picture, then folded over to protect the front of the picture and sent in a hard-backed envelope. A photo-caption story could be the entire release if the photo is good and there is not a great deal to report about it. For example, the story below could have come from a photo-caption release.

Trained to cope with emergencies

ANY emergency should be ably catered for by one of Princes Risborough Upper School's pupils.

The school has received a certificate for having now had 150 Year 12 pupils qualify for the St John Ambulance Three Cross Award as part of its Personal, Social and Health Education (PSHE) curriculum subject.

The awards combine the necessary skills – including treating heart attacks, choking and fractures – with giving pupils the ability to deal with situations with confidence.

In March, three of the newly trained pupils – Stephen Gough, Vanessa Rook and James Moore – put their skills to immediate use in a real-life situation to help a pensioner who fell and cut open her head.

Pictured with the Year 10 pupils receiving their two cross awards with merit are PSHE co-ordinator, Wendy Mason (centre back), headteacher Gaynor Hartle, and St John Ambulance Aylesbury district and area co-ordinators, Penny Earnshaw and Duncan Hammond, respectively.

Wolverton County School
School Road
Wolverton
Barsetshire
Tel: 01234 567890

PRESS RELEASE

PREMIER LEAGUE CAPTAIN REFEREES SCHOOL MATCH
Wolverton County kicks off season with one day football festival

(Date)

Wayne Philips, captain of Wolverton United premier league football team, refereed the final match at a one day football festival held by Wolverton County School on Saturday (date) to start the season. As part of the school's fund raising drive for new sports facilities, the event contributed over £300.

Teams from four neighbouring schools - Coppergate Grammar, St Olave's Boys School, Addenbridge High and Briar House - joined Wolverton County's footballers for a morning coaching session, followed by a knock out competition of 20-minute each-way matches.

Wolverton County won the hard fought final by 1-0. In an exciting second half, John McGregor of Wolverton County scored a goal eight minutes from the end, swiftly followed by a missed penalty by Coppergate Grammar.

Philips said: "All the teams were very keen. There's plenty of talent in school football. It's important for the future of the game that these youngsters get encouragement and good training. That's why I was pleased Wolverton County asked me to referee the match." At the end of the day he autographed shirts and footballs.

- ends -

For further information and photos of the match, contact:
Ian Martin, Deputy Head, Wolverton County School
Tel: 01234 567890

The sample press release above is better written and laid out than the one on the next page, so should be more effective.

53

Wolverton County School
School Road
Wolverton
Barsetshire
Tel: 01234 567890

Wolverton County wins final at football festival

The sports season opened in style on Saturday at Wolverton County School when its team won 1-0 against Coppergate College in a match that was guest-refereed by Wayne Philips, the captain of Wolverton United.

Wolverton County invited four neighbouring schools to a one day event to raise funds for new sports facilities. A morning coaching session was followed by a series of 20-minute each-way matches, culminating in a full length match between the semi-finalists.The hard fought match featured a goal-less first half, followed by a thrilling finale with a goal by McGregor of Wolverton County 8 minutes from the end, swiftly followed by a missed penalty by Coppergate Grammar.

Wayne was appearing at the invitation of the school. Spectators made a contribution of £1.00 each to watch the game, and afterwards Philips autographed shirts and footballs. In all, over £300 was raised. The Wolverton United team are supportive of school sports in the area and Philips commented: "Wolverton County has the makings of an excellent team. It's a tribute to the coaching at the school."

For further information contact Ian Martin, deputy head.

A poorly written, badly laid-out press release will not help your school's marketing effort

As always you need to know what your objective is in issuing the press release. Which readers are you aiming for? What is the main message you wish to convey to them? Assess your release in the light of these questions - is it likely to achieve your goals?

The person whose name appears at the bottom of the press release should be able to deal with queries arising from the release. Organisations which want their spokespeople to be as effective as possible in conveying their messages and being quoted accurately often send them on media training courses. Public relations consultancies should be able to suggest or may offer these courses. However they may be too expensive for many schools.

In the absence of media training the following guidelines should help you avoid the worst errors.

- Always ascertain in advance the journalist's name and publication and why they want to interview you.

- If you are not prepared, give an excuse and arrange to phone back within an agreed time, so you can prepare what you want to say about the subject. If you do not feel you can speak about the subject suggest someone who is better qualified so that the journalist regards you as helpful.

- Be sure to phone back, as agreed, to meet the journalist's deadline. If you are helpful and quotable the journalist will ask you to comment on educational issues again, which will help raise the school's profile.

- Never say anything to a journalist which you would regret seeing in print. Saying a statement is 'off the record' is no guarantee that the journalist will not use the information, particularly if you say 'off the record' retrospectively.

- When asking questions the journalist may lead the interview in a direction which does not help you, so you should try to keep control of the interview by knowing what message you want to convey and bringing the discussion back to what you want to say. Repeat your message several times in different ways to be sure the journalist cannot miss it - prepare two or three simple variations in advance and use some examples to illustrate your points. Some politicians are skilled at getting their message across and not answering questions unless they want to - listen to them being interviewed to discover how they steer the discussion.

- Use simple language. Do not use jargon or acronyms that are familiar to teachers but not to the general public - these days you're safe with 'GCSE' but when they were first introduced you would have needed to give an additional explanation that they were the exams replacing 'O' levels.

• Be positive in your comments and attitude - avoid making derogatory comments about other schools or educational issues; it is usually possible to turn a negative statement around by finding something positive to say about the converse side of the topic.

• Above all, do not lie!

You could arrange a role-playing session to give some practice to your spokespeople. Develop a couple of scenarios for the role-play. The first could be a situation which gives you an opportunity to put across some positive messages about the school; the second could be a more difficult interview where the journalist has unearthed some information which could damage the school if it becomes public. Make the scenarios as relevant as possible to your own school. Appoint someone to play the journalist who will be persistent in unearthing the facts and determined to pursue their own line of questioning. The spokesperson and journalist should prepare individually in advance: then the role-playing should take place before some observers who can comment afterwards on any areas where the spokesperson was effective and others where lessons can be learnt. A audio or video recording of the role play could also help when going over answers and considering how performance could be improved. If you have any parents or governors with experience in public relations or journalism ask if they will help.

Role-play scenario

Fred Smith is a teacher at Easystart Primary School which has recently had a few instances of bullying. This is Fred's second job since leaving college. He is introduced to a local journalist, Bob

Jones, on a social occasion eg. at a party or in the pub. Before the role play begins Fred should have been given guidelines for dealing with the media (see page 55) and have had time to absorb them.

The person playing the part of the journalist will be given the following brief:

You are to play the role of Bob Jones, an ambitious young journalist who regards every conversation as an opportunity to unearth a news story. By being chatty and friendly you should attempt to obtain information in an apparently casual way. You meet Fred Smith on a social occasion and learn that he is a teacher at Easystart Primary School. You have heard that Easystart Primary has had some problems with bullying but you need confirmation and any additional facts with which to approach the headteacher for an interview. Your objective on meeting Fred is to get this confirmation and any other useful facts.

The conversation might go something like this:

Bob: So you were at college with John *(their mutual friend)*. What are you doing now?

Fred: I'm a teacher. How about you?

Bob: I'm a reporter on the Easystart Gazette. It must be pretty tough being a teacher these days. What do you teach - primary or secondary?

Fred: I've just begun at Easystart Primary. I'm enjoying it - it's nowhere near as tough as my last school. I'm quite happy to take football after school here, but I wasn't so keen there - you never knew if the lads were carrying knives or would gang up and get violent - even if they were only ten year olds.

Bob: You're a footballer then? (Fred nods assent) I used to play but I'm an armchair player now. Of course, I love going to live matches too.

Bob recounts some anecdotes and talks about sport for a while then ends up asking some questions about Fred's involvement in football at the school so that Fred feels quite relaxed when Bob carries on.

Bob: One of my friends has a boy at Easystart - he had a really bad time being bullied at one stage. I think it's been sorted out now. Mind, I don't know how you handle that sort of the thing. How do you deal with it?

Fred (enjoying the chance to show off a little): I won't stand for it in my class. *(explains how he deals with bullies)*

Bob: I think my friends threatened to withdraw their son before anything was done. Is there an overall policy or is it just up to each teacher to sort out problems as they arise?

Fred: I'm not really sure.

Bob: But haven't you been told what the policy is?

Fred: Not yet, but I am new this year.

Bob: Yes, but surely if there is a policy you'd have been told by now wouldn't you? After all it is half way through the year isn't it?

Fred: Well yes, I suppose so.

Bob: Still you seem to know what to do - have you had to put it into practice much?

Fred: A few times.

Bob: I suppose that was at you previous school?

Fred: Mostly - as I said it was a pretty tough school.

Bob leads the conversation on to Fred's job at the previous school.

Bob: It must have been difficult. Was it your first job out of college?

Fred: Yes - a real baptism by fire.

Bob: But it sounds as if there are some problem cases at Easystart too. You said most of the bullying was at your last school - so some obviously must still be happening at Easystart. Are there very many cases?

Fred: Not really.

Bob: I suppose after your last school it must be pretty easy to deal with?

Fred: It has helped.

Bob: So you've had some cases since coming to Easystart?

Fred: Well, nothing much really.

Bob: But this is only your second school, isn't it? *(Fred nods in assent)*

Bob: And you said mostly you'd dealt with bullies at the last school which must mean you've dealt with at least one here?

Fred: Well yes.

Bob: And, I take it, you were just expected to use your previous experience as a basis for dealing with it?

Fred: The deputy head backed me up.

Bob: It still seems strange that there's no overall policy to help - teachers have a hard enough job as it is without having to decide their own methods for dealing with each and every problem.

Fred: It is quite a load with all the preparation and so forth.

Bob (exuding sympathy): People never seem to realise how much extra work teachers have to do - I've got friends who are up till all hours marking work or preparing lessons - and they keep thinking about school and reading and collecting things during their holidays. I hope Easystart gives you a bit more help in other areas.

Bob could continue the conversation to find out about other areas in which support is lacking at Easystart - he has in effect been told that Easystart still has bullies but has no policy for dealing with them. With this information he can approach the head teacher for comment saying that a source has told him there is no policy on how to deal with bullies but the school still has a bullying problem. And of course journalists never reveal their sources.

Role-play scenario 2

Anne Runcorn is the head teacher of Failsway Comprehensive School which is located in an an inner city area where students come from a mixture of backgrounds. For many, English is not their mother tongue - 20 different mother tongues are listed; a high proportion of the students are from single parent families or families where both parents are registered as unenmployed. Failsway has recently had poor results in the exam results league tables. It has also undergone an OFSTED inspection.

The person playing the part of the journalist, Bob Jones, will be given the following brief:

You have heard that there is dissatisfaction among parents about the standard of teaching in maths and science. The results back up the parents' view but the OFSTED report's comments on teaching standards does not support it. You want to find out the truth, which you suspect is poor teaching, and learn if the head is prepared to fire poor teachers.

Some questions Bob Jones might ask are:

• Failsway Comprehensive performed poorly in the exam leagues table, I'm sure you'd agree. It slipped two percentage points in the proportion of GCSE student obtaining five passes at Grade C or above. This must provide cause for concern - wouldn't you agree?

• What factors do you consider to be responsible for these poor results?

• One factor must surely be poor teaching. How are you addressing that problem?

- What were your first actions on reading the OFSTED report on the school?

- Social factors cannot be wholly to blame. After all, at Rottenborough School - just across the county boundary - there's a similar mix of backgrounds but the results are above the national average. They are obviously doing something right that isn't happening here. Can you explain that?

- Have you asked any teachers to leave because they are not up to the job?

- Would you do so, if necessary?

- Surely the current results show that this is necessary?

- Have you any plans to recruit new teaching staff?

- Have you budgeted for any teacher training in the coming year?

- Are you introducing any new schemes to boost staff morale and improve motivation?

Anne Runcorn should think of all the possible difficult questions before the interview and prepare to answer them honestly, stressing anything positive and not dwelling on negatives - instead mentioning actions aimed at improving matters in future.

Target suitable media

Which are the appropriate media to send a release to? So far I've mentioned local newspapers, TV and radio. You can obtain the names of editors of most publications from media directories but for the school's limited needs it is not worth investing in one of these - they are issued every month because editors and publications come and go; a single issue costs over £200 and will soon be out of date. If any parents at the school work in public relations they will undoubtedly have access to such directories so ask them to produce a list of relevant press (names, addresses, telephone and fax numbers) to use as a start. If not, look for the contact phone number in your local papers and phone them and ask for the editor to establish the best person to contact - you may need to direct news items and diary information to different people. If you send the release to the correct individual there is more chance it will be used. It is also worthwhile making a follow up phone call to check that the release has been received and ask if any further details are needed, if extra pictures are needed (assuming you have them) or to enable the paper's photographer to arrange to come to the school to take photos. If your school choir has made a recording send a release about it to the local papers but include a

☐ **Tarporley High**

Head gets in a lather for charity fund razor

TARPORLEY High head of sixth form David Robinson is feeling a bit sore around the chin – all in the cause of charity.

Unknown to him *Chronicle* photographer Gerry Lockley had been invited to witness the public scraping of his beard by two of the school's staff.

It all started with the sixth form committee.

Mr Robinson explained: 'Somehow or other I agreed to have my beard shaved off, provided the sixth form raised £300.

'Perhaps it was the onset of half-term that prompted this rash gesture.

'Twenty odd years with a beard is a long time but I hope my suffering will have helped to bring some comfort to others.'

The sixth formers exceeded their target by more then £100' and in all the school raised £733.

CHIN TRIM: Teacher David Robinson looks in a hairy situation as deputy head Julia Gilchrist, armed with hedge trimmer, and lunchtime supervisor Barbara Steele get ready to shave off his beard.   1333L26A review copy of the recording when sending the release to the local radio station. It may just be tempted to play it. If the school has an Internet connection you may be tempted to use that as a vehicle for getting positive messages out - though it's uncertain at present just whom they would reach - and therefore is probably not yet worth the effort (See also p. 100).

Make sure that you get all events publicised in the diary columns in the local press: open days or evenings for prospective parents and pupils, car boot sales, jumble sales and other public fund raising events. You will need to check press deadlines for receipt of such information and make sure it arrives in plenty of time. Send the information as a press release.

If you have a photo of last year's fair or fundraising event send it (the more unusual and entertaining it is, the better).

While local papers may make room for some local success or human interest stories, the national press is unlikely to be interested in most schools unless a disaster or scandal occurs. That is when you need to know how to deal with a crisis.

Crisis management

You seek press coverage to raise your school's profile in a positive way but if the media spotlight turns on the school for an unwelcome reason you will you suddenly find yourself trying to escape the glare. What steps will you take to reduce press interest rapidly rather than allowing it to escalate out of proportion? You can plan for the unexpected so that you and your staff will be able to react more calmly in a situation which could otherwise cause you to panic and perhaps make the wrong decisions. Think of any problems or incidents which could occur in your school and be exaggerated or damage the school's reputation if they become known to a journalist. Truancy, poor exam results, bullying, drugs, sex education issues, teenage pregnancies, racial prejudice, vandalism, safety in sports activities and other areas of school life, real or hoax bomb scares, arson, a school minibus accident, teachers being physically abused, student rioting and violence do not all occur in every school but just one such incident could bring the press to your door. A school with the best of reputations will interest the press if they learn that exam results have not been up to previously high standards in a particular year.

Having identified any issues that could relate to your school, decide how you would react to possible press queries. At such a time it is even more important to adhere to your media relations policy and only allow authorised spokespeople to respond to press queries. A sensible precaution is to have a suitable statement ready for a number of eventualities. It can be used as an initial response, allowing you time to investigate what has happened and then issue further statements in a controlled manner. The press will be interested in what has happened, why it has happened and what you are going to do about it, so those are the questions you should be prepared to answer during any crisis.

The press may learn of some events before you do - for example an accident involving students or staff way from the school premises - in which case you can say you will investigate and tell them to expect a further statement from you. Make sure that you adhere to the time even if it is necessary to provide another holding statement until the situation is under control. If there has been a fire, for example, it may be some time before the reasons are known. The press will continue to be interested if they think anything is being hidden from them so keep them informed on a regular basis. In such a situation if arson is suspected by someone with a grudge against the school you may have to dispel all sorts of rumours. A clear statement that the police are investigating the matter and until the investigation is complete you will not speculate on the outcome but you will tell them the result as soon as you know it, may be enough to dampen their interest for the moment. You may need to issue further statements during the progress of the investigation and when you know the result make sure you inform the press before they find out from some other source. Then you will be able to issue the information in the way that best preserves your reputation. Contingency planning, done in advance, will repay the time and effort involved in these circumstances.

Sometimes facts which you would prefer not to publicise may become known, for example high truancy figures at the school. In this case you will need to be able to explain why they are high at present and what is being done to prevent truancy. If in your response you can justifiably suggest that the current situation is exceptional and you can then list plenty of remedial actions, the facts may prove less damaging than they would otherwise.

Obviously the media are not the only people who will be interested in a crisis and what is being done about it. You need to inform the whole school community - staff, students and parents - about events as they unfold. It is important to gauge people's emotional reaction to any crisis and respond sensitively. People may be angry about truancy rates and falling standards or anxious and grief stricken after an accident. You will need to show that you understand people's feelings and respond appropriately.

Chapter 6
Sponsorship

You will have often seen or heard a weather report, road traffic bulletin or sports event sponsored by a commercial company. The sponsor's name is prominently displayed or mentioned and the players wear heavily branded clothes. These are just some of the more obvious examples of a promotional tool that is now almost as inescapable as advertising. For many companies, sponsorship is an accepted part of their marketing mix and commands a substantial share of the budget.

For most schools, however, with their limited resources, sponsorship is less likely to be a marketing tool than an opportunity to obtain additional funding. The scale of sponsorship varies. Whether your school needs new books or an entire new building for the library, finding a sponsor is one way of meeting the cost.

Many organisations are keen to imprint their brand names on the minds of children and their parents, but often the benefits sponsors seek are more subtle than mere brand awareness. Some companies want to gain kudos from an association with the event or object they sponsor. Others recognise the value of contributing to schools to help develop a well-educated workforce and benefit society as a whole. Even so, you will need to devote considerable time, effort and imagination to finding sponsors, since schools are just one of many worthy causes competing for a share in businesses' sponsorship budgets.

Depending on the level of funding you are aiming to achieve, you may need to assign a member of staff to seeking sponsorship full time for six months or a year, or to appoint an external fund raiser. The investment should be well worthwhile. You may have the help of a parent or governor with suitable experience but unless you are lucky enough to have a willing volunteer who has recently retired, it is unlikely they will have enough time for the task. Instead they could support the staff member assigned to raising sponsorship with their ideas and advice. The person you want should have resilience and perseverance, since they will meet with plenty of rebuffs, together with the ability to recognise commercial needs and deal professionally with senior executives of large companies. A positive, outgoing personality is essential.

Seeking sponsorship

The association between sponsor and sponsored should be mutually beneficial. In seeking a sponsor, consider the likely objectives of the companies you approach and what your school has to offer that will match their needs. For example, your school may be a centre of excellence in art, sport or technology. Manufacturers or retailers of art materials, sports equipment or computer software products may value a link with the school because of its reputation in their line of business.

Even if your school does not have such a distinction, if it has excellent teachers in a particular discipline but lacks facilities, you may be able to interest a sponsor in funding the facilities needed to gain a specialist reputation. At the very least, the sponsor should gain publicity from contributing to educational improvement.

When it comes to reasons that a company would want to sponsor your school, think as broadly as possible. Your school may not have distinctive educational strengths but its location could be a selling point to certain companies. For example, if it is in the centre of a heavily congested inner city area - often seen as a form of deprivation - it will probably be close to the offices of some large companies which have a policy of fostering good relationships with their local community. Equally, you could interest companies which have a message to convey about their contribution to relieving urban congestion, such as local or national bus and train companies. (They will also see the school and surrounding community as larger than average users of public transport, a potential source of revenue.) Don't let an approach to public transport providers prevent you from considering companies with a vested interest in private transport, at least until a relationship has been formed. Car manufacturers and petrol companies may be keen to promote their attempts to reduce pollution in the inner city.

If your school is in a rural area, you too could approach these companies but from a different standpoint, since rural communities rely heavily on private transport. And you can target a different set of possible sponsors - companies such as suppliers of agrochemicals and farm machinery, or large local employers with an interest in maintaining high local educational standards to ensure a well educated future workforce. If the school is in an area of natural beauty, companies keen to promote their work in conserving and protecting the environment may value an association with it.

While the effort involved in obtaining sponsorship should not be underestimated, you can reduce the burden by approaching it in an organised way. A first port of call should be those bodies that could introduce you to businesses interested in sponsorship, such as your local Training and Enterprise Council (TEC) and the local Education Business Partnership. Contact your local Chamber of Commerce as well - a list of local businesses may reveal names you would not have known about and increase your chance of obtaining sponsorship for a variety of activities. Firstly, approach those companies you know are interested in sponsoring education. After that the flow-chart below will help you prioritise other companies to target, according to your needs and attributes.

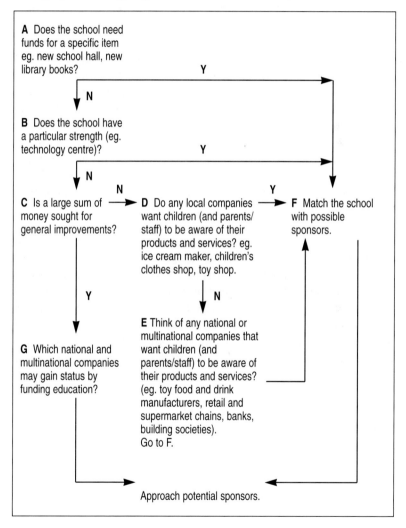

A Does the school need funds for a specific item eg. new school hall, new library books?

Y →

↓ N

B Does the school have a particular strength (eg. technology centre)?

Y →

↓ N

C Is a large sum of money sought for general improvements? → **D** Do any local companies want children (and parents/staff) to be aware of their products and services? eg. ice cream maker, children's clothes shop, toy shop. Y → **F** Match the school with possible sponsors.

↓ Y ↓ N

G Which national and multinational companies may gain status by funding education?

E Think of any national or multinational companies that want children (and parents/staff) to be aware of their products and services? (eg. toy food and drink manufacturers, retail and supermarket chains, banks, building societies).
Go to F.

Approach potential sponsors.

Begin by deciding your sponsorship objectives. If, for example, you have a specific requirement for a new school building, the process of matching your needs to possible sponsors will immediately rule out companies too small to donate the substantial sum this would entail. You would need to consider national and multinational companies, but it would probably be most effective to approach those with a head office, regional office, factory, or large branch in your area. Alternatively, you could attempt to bring together a consortium of local companies in the building trade with a local architect and suggest a co-operative effort which would give them a showpiece for their work.

If, on the other hand, your school needs funds for a wide variety of items from library books to new sports equipment, you could prioritise the items and match each one to suitable individual companies and obtain a range of sponsors - or direct all your efforts toward obtaining funds to cover everything from a major company that would gain status as a 'good citizen' or 'good neighbour' by funding education.

Success is most likely if you think about the likely objectives of the companies you approach and what your school has to offer that will match their needs. Organisations such as toy shops, toy manufacturers, soft drink manufacturers, fast food chains, book shops, banks and building societies all see children as potential customers, so their interest may be greatest in sponsoring items that pupils want such as playground equipment, awards, prizes and school journeys. Sponsored items that reach a wider audience of parents and the local community will appeal to other companies. For example a tour operator or hotel chain might fund a school theatre production or at least the programme so that its name becomes known to an adult audience in a positive context, while a local insurance company or estate agent might sponsor a school prospectus that is seen by many adults living near or interested in living near the school.

You should try to match the item you want sponsored with the nature of the sponsor's business. For example, if you want a company to provide funds for a sporting event you could try the local branch of a national sports goods shop or shoe shop which sells sports shoes as part of its range. If the local shop cannot help you find out where its head office and factories are located. A phone call should enable you to establish who at head office is responsible for sponsorship, or at least for marketing. If not, find out who the managing director is. Always send letters to a named individual so that you can follow your letter with a phone call to initiate a discussion and perhaps arrange a meeting.

When you approach the companies, by letter or phone, help them perceive sponsorship of your school as an opportunity by suggesting a benefit they will gain by being a sponsor. Ask for a meeting to discuss the matter further so you can give them a fuller understanding of the school. Invite them to visit the school to explore other areas that could be of mutual benefit.

Draft a standard letter which can be slightly adapted for each company you approach.

Dear

Sponsorship opportunity

I am writing to invite Trinket Toys Limited to form an association with Eager Beavers Primary School which educates the largest group of children aged five or eleven in the community where your head office/factory is located.

We are currently seeking sponsorship for a range of items and activities. For example we need new playground equipment. Many children and their parents will undoubtedly remember any donation to this cause with gratitude. Obviously, should you choose to help us, we would be pleased to provide suitable recognition for your generosity.

I would welcome an opportunity to meet you to discuss the matter further and consider ways in which an association between your company and the school could provide mutual benefit. I will telephone you shortly to arrange a suitable appointment.

71

Another approach might be along these lines:

```
Dear
Sponsorship opportunity

Bloggs County School is a mixed comprehensive school
which educates students of all abilities in an area of
high unemployment. We are currently seeking sponsorship
of £50,000 to build a new school hall. This will for
the first time enable the whole school to meet togeth-
er for assembly, as well as providing a much needed
communal area for many other school events. It will
also be available to the wider community for many
activities outside of school hours. It will therefore
provide a highly valued resource in a severely deprived
area.
    I feel sure that XYZ Company as a major employer in
the area, which is renowned for its generosity to the
less privileged groups in society, will be interested
in learning more about the school and its needs with a
possible view to sponsoring this major programme or
some of our other requirements.
    I will telephone you shortly to arrange a suitable
time to discuss the matter more fully.
```

You may think of including a school brochure with the letter but that would be a waste of valuable resources. It would be better to save the brochure for further contact with companies that show a glimmering of interest in the school.

Your letters may produce an immediate negative reply. If this happens you may simply decide to pursue other possibilities but it is probably worth phoning to establish what the company's attitude is to sponsorship. You may learn that sponsorship is against company policy which will save you wasting time in future or you could discover that this year's budget has been used up but open a discussion that will lead to consideration when next year's plans are being developed, or at least allow you to maintain contact to see if the situation changes.

If you prefer to try direct contact by phone first, do so. Letters can save time if you need to approach a lot of companies for relatively small donations and they provide an introductory gambit when you phone. You should phone all the companies you write to unless they have replied with an outright indication that sponsorship is not company policy.

Having arranged a meeting you need to prepare well, presenting the school and its requirement in the best possible light. Be flexible in presenting information about the school. If it is apparent that the people you meet are more interested in visiting the school to see it for themselves, arrange a visit rather than prolong the initial presentation unnecessarily.

Once you form a relationship with a sponsor it will preclude deals with competitors or even competing interest groups. Before approaching any organisation, decide whether you will be comfortable defending a link with it, in view of its likely objectives and its general reputation with the public. You will have to explain the relationship to parents, the local press and possibly even the national press. Obviously the sponsor will support you in this.

You will also need to consider the interest of your sponsor if the relationship is to prosper. It would hardly be tactful to buy supplies from your sponsor's competitors when you have a choice. Such matters need to be discussed at the outset of the relationship. Sometimes sponsors want some control over the nature and style of whatever they are sponsoring, though this is not always the case. You should agree any conditions of the sponsorship during negotiation about the exact nature of the deal and have them written into the contract.

Although you may have done some research to try to establish the objectives of the company you meet, discussion will almost certainly reveal others. You need to be alert to new possibilities and remain open to suggestions from the sponsors. In this way you are more likely to develop a relationship which will continue and benefit both your school and the sponsor.

Try and involve your sponsor(s) in as many aspects of school life as possible. Sponsors may be able to provide work experience placements, offer innovative training sessions for staff, provide additional interest at events for parents and if you have a major sponsor you could invite your main contact to become a school governor. Such activities will foster the relationship and enable both parties to recognise opportunities they can gain from it. Sponsorship can provide rich rewards for schools prepared to put in the necessary effort to find sponsors and to be innovative in their work with them.

Parent and staff involvement

Sponsorship can be a positive benefit to schools. But care needs to be taken to ensure that sensitivities amongst parents and staff are met.

It is very important that the school's staff are fully aware of the potential of sponsorship, and that they are supportive of the exercise. It only takes one comment from an unconvinced staff member to wreck a delicate relationship. To make sure that the staff are behind the initiative, you will need to invest time in explaining the need, and discussing the potential for sponsorship with the whole staff, preferably at an after-school meeting in a relaxed atmosphere. In this forum, objections should be freely raised and discussed. For example, some people may consider certain sponsors inappropriate, while others have a different list. It will prove impossible to accommodate everyone's agenda! Try and bring all this out in the open: it is far better to be aware of concerns from the outset than to discover them once a sponsorship relationship has been established. You may discover that there are other, more suitable funding avenues to explore. And it is simply good management practice to take the staff along with you in this kind of venture.

Similarly with parents. Information and openness are the keys. Some parents may not like the idea of 'their' school being associated with the world of commerce: the idea of sponsorship may galvanise the PTA into activity. Or, more constructively, you may well find that parents are an excellent source of ideas, suggestions and help, once they are convinced that you are approaching sponsorship in a responsible, rational and constructive way. In any case, they should hear about potential sponsorship from the school rather than from the newspapers, and there should be an opportunity for discussion, eg. at a parents' evening. A policy of openness and consultation will repay many times the effort it costs.

Chapter 7
Advertising

O rganisations can place their message before the public in the exact words and style they choose by advertising. Whereas press relations activity cannot guarantee press coverage, advertising gives complete control over the content and appearance of the message because the organisation pays for the space and for creative staff to develop the words and graphics in the advertisement. The only limits are those imposed by the Advertising Standards Authority and by the size of the advertising budget.

Before advertising you should consider what your objectives are and whether there is any other way of achieving them. If there is, you will need to determine which method is likely to be most suitable and cost effective for each of your requirements. If your budget allows, you may decide to use a combination of promotional techniques. For example, advertising could be used to reinforce some recent good press coverage.

When advertising you need to choose the most appropriate medium to reach your chosen audience. If you want local people to know about the school you could create an advertisement to use in a direct mail campaign and in local newspapers. You could also consider advertising some events on local radio, bearing in mind the cost both of the advertising time and of having the ad made. If yours is an independent boarding school, seeking pupils from a wide area, you will need to advertise in regional or national publications such as the education supplements of the national press.

Whatever the medium, you can be more certain that your ads will gain attention and work well if you select an experienced supplier such as an advertising agency or a designer to create the advertisement. However for some events like school fairs which you want lots of local people to attend and which have an image of informality and fun, you may achieve a suitable result without professional help. Try using the school's desktop publishing facilities and ask students to create a leaflet. Specify the details that must be included and then hold a competition or perhaps have the leaflet included in an art or design project.

What makes a good advertisement?

Effective advertisements fulfil a number of functions which can be grouped together to give the mnemonic, AIDA. These are:

A - attract the attention of the people at whom they are aimed

I - gain their interest

D- make them desire the product or service being advertised - or at least desire to know more about it

A - cause them to take action either by buying the product or learning more about it.

AIDA provides a useful guideline for the creation of advertisements. It is also important to remember that advertising copy should stick to facts not opinion. People trust advertisements less than editorial, so may be unwilling to believe opinions given in them. But they can check facts, so by including selected facts which benefit the school's image, your advertisement can inspire confidence. This fifth factor can be added to AIDA for guidance in creating good advertisements.

The overall appearance of an advertisement, which is the combined effect of the layout, design, typography and visual elements such as a map, photo or diagram, contributes to its effectiveness. If the school has a well established logo and a specific house style which is used throughout its publications, this can be carried into its advertising. It would be best to employ a designer to develop a style for the complete range of materials, including the different types of advertisement the school may wish to use. If a style is developed for recruitment ads and another for advertisements for events it may be possible to re-use the same basic ad on a number of occasions by judicious editing of the text. However care must be taken to ensure that the ads do not deteriorate by becoming cluttered and changing too much from the original design concept.

If photos are used they should be of good quality, showing a scene that is lively and interesting. The school may have some good quality photos available if it has invested in them for its prospectus. More information about photos is contained later in this chapter. Seek the advice of a designer when introducing photos and other graphic devices to advertisements. If you only have a small advertising budget, you may have to omit photos. It is best to spend money on good design. If you are lucky you may find that one of the parents is in design or advertising and is willing to help.

The language in an advertisement should appeal directly to the reader. By addressing the reader personally and using short simple words which are familiar and easy to understand, a well-worded advertisement can involve the reader. The use of action words, especially active rather than passive verbs, gives immediacy and helps create interest. Consider the difference in effect of the following pairs of words or phrases:

wanted	required
we are looking for...	a vacancy exists within our organisation for....
visit us on our open day	you are invited to visit
come and see us in action	there will be an opportunity to view the school at work

The words on the left have a personal or emotional appeal and can be immediately understood; those on the right are more formal in tone and use an unnecessary number of words which to some extent obscures the meaning. It is best to avoid this type of conventional business language. Simplicity, clarity and directness are far more effective, not only in advertising but also in other forms of communication.

Advertisements should not be expected to sell a product or service. Many ads include far too much additional text that detracts from the overall appearance and interferes with the immediate message that should be conveyed to the reader. Think exactly what you want the ad to achieve - for example, to attract people to a school open day - and focus on that single objective in creating the ad. Selling the school, persuading people that it offers a good education or is a good place to work, should be reserved for the event or interview itself.

The AIDA principle (attract attention, gain interest, create desire, provoke action) which lies behind good advertisements can be illustrated by looking at recruitment advertising. If you are advertising for a teacher you must ensure that teachers will notice your ad. Depending on the type of teacher you need, you will advertise in the education press or in a specialist subject publication and perhaps also in the local press. Although the post being

Differing styles of school advertisements: the Avenue House School ad attracts attention by using a photograph, but the head's name is larger than the educational detail. Below, the Southfields College ad has been professionally designed, using a logo: the boxed text emphasises recent changes, and the successes are listed. It is eyecatching and clearly laid out. The Gunnersbury School ad clearly communicates its grant-maintained status and the open day dates, but is not very clear or eyecatching. This selection illustrates that results may be dictated by available budget.

advertised is the same, the ads for each publication should be different.

In the education press your ad will undoubtedly be targeted at the correct people but it will be competing for their attention with many other ads. To ensure that potential candidates notice your ad, you must focus on whatever is unique or particularly attractive about the job or the school, so the majority of readers will stop to read more. Feedback from past recruitment campaigns should give you some idea of what attracts teachers to your school. It may be the idyllic location, the challenge of working in an inner city area, the multi-ethnic mix of the school, its academic ethos or the high profile of the job itself which will grab their attention. Once readers have noticed the ad and decided it is relevant, they will read further to discover more about the job. This is the point where the ad must create interest by describing some more good points about the school or the job. You need to provide enough information for people to be interested and want to know more, so they feel this could be the right job (you have then created desire). They will take action by phoning for an application form if you include the necessary contact details. The task of selling the job to them if they are the right candidate should happen at the interview; it is not the job of the advertisement.

If the school is in a populous area where a number of teachers live, some of whom may be considering a change of job, you could advertise in the situations vacant section of the local newspaper. Then your ad would have to stand out among ads for cooks, builders, secretaries and miscellaneous other jobs. So the words which would have to leap from the page to grab the attention of all teachers in the area would be 'TEACHER WANTED' or something similar. Once the ad had caught their attention you would then have to interest them in the school and the job so that they would phone for an application form if they were suitably qualified. Obviously there is less chance of reaching so many suitably qualified teachers by this route but if any do live in the area they may be more interested in the job than those living a long way off who would have difficulty commuting or would have to relocate.

Similarly, if you were to use a specialist publication, such as a scientific journal when recruiting a science teacher, you would have to make teaching the immediate focus of attention in the ad.

If you are seeking to attract prospective parents to an open day or evening you should give just enough information to make them want to come and see the school; they can find out more at the open day, which is your opportunity to sell the school. Examples of these type of advertisements are on p. 80.

Proof reading

To meet the deadline of the publication in which you are advertising, be sure to allow sufficient time for proof reading (and corrections, if necessary) once the advertisement has been set. Check thoroughly for typographical errors. Commonly known as typos, these are spelling mistakes which occur during typesetting. There is nothing worse than a school advertising its high academic standards below a name which is wrongly spelt. It may have been a typo but it is your responsibility to spot it and have it corrected before going to press; the public will simply see it as a careless spelling mistake by the school and this will detract from attempts to build the school's reputation for quality and excellence. (A selection of the most used proof-reading symbols and their meanings are shown on p. 96)

Few images or phrases are so memorable that people recall them after only seeing them once. For this reason repetition is one of the essentials of successful advertising. Your advertisement will be more effective in helping the school build its image and maintain a high profile if it is repeated periodically. Some schools may choose to remain in the public eye by advertising regularly throughout the year. Others will focus on specific events. For example schools should advertise in every issue of their local papers for a couple of months before their open days or evenings. If regular advertising is too expensive, the advertising campaigns for specific events can be reinforced by public relations activity for the rest of the year.

Managing the school's advertising

One person should be responsible for managing the school's advertising. Whoever the job falls to should identify the school's long term objectives and short term priorities with regard to its advertising. You should decide how the advertising budget for the year will be spent. When assessing the cost of advertising you will have to include the cost of creating the advertisement as well as the media cost and allocate sufficient resources to accomplish specific advertising objectives. You may find the budget cannot be stretched to include some low priority projects and you will need to discuss how these objectives can be achieved by other methods, in consultation with other members of staff who are involved in marketing the school.

When you need a supplier ask your LEA, PTA or other local contacts if they can recommend someone suitable; develop a shortlist after seeing some of their previous work; provide them with a written brief about what you require, and then they can submit a written quotation from which you will make your final decision.

You will learn from experience which advertisements work best and where your ads have most success. This learning will only come if you evaluate your advertising campaigns. For example, always find out how people learned about an open day or a job vacancy. If they ring to ask for an application form, ensure that your office staff ask where they learned about the school and keep a record of the information. You may need to spend some time establishing a formal structure for obtaining such details or the school may already have an evaluation scheme that covers advertising, events, publications and public relations activity. By vetting this information you will soon see whether a particular newspaper is the best source for recruiting staff or brings most prospective parents to open days/evenings.

Finally, always be on the look out for new ideas. There are plenty of advertisements around. Start noticing which ones attract your attention and why. You may find some ideas that can be applied to the school. Talk about them with your supplier. Unless new ideas are tried and tested, you will never know if they could prove useful.

Chapter 8
Publications

There is a statutory requirement for all maintained schools to publish a prospectus giving a substantial amount of information about their performance, admissions, absences, the curriculum, organisation of education and teaching methods at the school, details of sex education and religious education policies, careers guidance, provision for children with special educational needs, routes taken by pupils over the age of 16, complaints procedures and so forth. You will no doubt be familiar with the detailed requirements set out in Circular 14/94, *The Parent's Charter: Publication of Information about Secondary School Performance* in 1994 or Circular 15/94, the primary school equivalent, and subsequent letters updating some of the content.

The governing bodies of LEA-maintained schools can ask their LEA to publish their prospectus, but they must still provide the necessary information, so they cannot escape the arduous task of gathering, preparing and checking it to ensure that all the figures and details published are accurate. If prospectuses are simply filled with text and tables that meet statutory requirements the task for parents of ploughing through a mass of detail about several schools in an effort to compare them can be daunting. By investing some extra time and money schools can considerably enhance their image and impress potential customers by publishing a prospectus which presents information in a clear and attractive manner that entices people to read it.

There are a number of stages in producing any publication. Various people and suppliers will be involved at different stages but one person should be given overall responsibility for seeing the publication through the entire process from preparing copy to having the publication printed. This person - let us call him or her the production editor - will need the ability to manage one or two suppliers and to commission written and visual material, ensuring that it is provided on time. Editorial skills are needed to prepare text for typesetting and to proof read and correct the pages once they have been typeset. If no member of staff has this skill a well qualified parent with time to spare may be able to help. Or the entire production of the publication could be contracted to an outside company such as a PR consultancy, a writing or design agency.

In order to commission outside suppliers it is necessary to understand the entire process. The production editor should know the school's objective in producing the publication in order to decide what content to include and ways in which the content can be conveniently divided into sections to assist the reader. This can be discussed at an early stage with the designer who should be able to contribute useful ideas and suggest ways of dividing and laying out the material so that it is easy to assimilate, as well as providing overall design elements which unify the publication.

The production editor commissions different people to provide each element of the publication:
• written copy (text and tables of statistics)
• graphics, pictures, photos
• design
• printing.

Words

The production editor may well be the person who writes the text for the publication. Methods vary. Some people prefer to write the text in full as their starting point so that the designer knows exactly how much space to allow for it. Others write the text to fit the space available in the layout. Obviously the space has to be sufficient to contain all the material required by statute.

The writing style should be clear and simple. Where there is an alternative it is usually better to use a short word rather than a long one, for example 'need' not 'require'. Take care to avoid ambiguity; if in doubt, re-read a sentence later to be sure you have conveyed what you meant, or ask someone else to read it and check they have understood what you intended. Also avoid using words imprecisely, for example 'continual' and 'continuous' are not interchangeable; be sure the meaning is clear. Watch out for unnecessary repetition, such as 'he also went too', for archaic words, such as 'whilst' which sound stilted, and for over-used words and phrases, particularly those which are currently fashionable, such as 'ongoing', which are unimaginative and will soon seem dated.

Here are some examples of wordy and concise text:

School societies include a wide variety of sports clubs including netball, hockey, football, rounders, tennis and rugby. There are a wide range of extra curricular activities which include an environmental society, a computer club, homework clubs, a choir, a school band, and a home economics group. There are also a wide range of fund raising activities for charity. *(58 words)*

Extra-curricular societies include various sports clubs, such as netball, hockey, football, rounders, tennis and rugby; an environmental society; a computer club; homework clubs; a choir; a band, and a home economics group.

There are also many fund raising activities for charity. *(42 words)*

The paragraph has been reduced from 58 words to 42. In context, following a section on compulsory sports tuition, it is apparent that the sporting activities here are not part of the curriculum so all the activities mentioned are extra-curricular. The revision avoids repeating 'include' and 'there are a wide range of'. And by altering the final sentence there is no need to decide whether to use the singular or plural verb with the collective noun 'range'.

The school policy is to make no charge in respect of books and equipment provided in connection with the National Curriculum. *(21 words)*

The school does not charge for books and equipment needed for National Curriculum subjects. *(14 words)*

All pupils are involved in the preparation of a Record of Personal Achievement. *(13 words)*

All pupils prepare a Record of Personal Achievement. *(8 words)*

Watch out for phrases like 'in respect of', 'in connection with', 'the provision of', 'involved in' which can usually be replaced by a single word.

If a number of people have contributed various sections of copy the editor will almost certainly have to rewrite sections to ensure consistency and conform to house style. House style should be maintained throughout all the school's publications. It covers the use of alternatives such as 'organise' or 'organize'; singular or plural verbs where their subject is a collective noun eg. 'the school/company/group is' or 'the school/company/group are'; use of initial capitals - generally it is preferable to avoid unnecessary capital letters; rules for indenting paragraphs; how to write numbers (usually they are written in full up to ten and figures are used thereafter); abbreviations eg. Limited or Ltd., High Street or High St. and so on. If your school has not instituted a house style, make it a priority to develop one. You may be able to obtain a basic style from a local printer or publisher and then add to it, as specific items relating to the school occur. The editor will also have to make sure that spelling and grammar are correct throughout and that suitable punctuation is used to make the meaning clear.

Graphics and pictures

Visual interest is created by the addition of graphic elements which break up the text, make sections readily identifiable and create areas on each page on which the eye will focus.

Photos are an obvious way of creating visual interest. However they must be good quality photographs. The subject should be relevant, probably showing members of the school involved in some activity where they look lively and interested. Employ a professional photographer to be sure you get suitable photographs, unless you have an exceptionally talented amateur photographer on the staff or among the parents. Even professional photographers specialise in particular types of photography so don't employ a landscape photographer if you want photos of active people.

Often amateur photographs do not have the sharpness or well balanced composition that is needed. Sometimes a photographer may catch a fleeting moment and get just the right photo, but more often a good photo has to be created. The composition of the photograph is important - the subject should be clearly visible, being well lit and standing out from the background. The background may provide a contrast but usually should not be too noticeable. Fussy cluttered backgrounds distract. Designers can crop photos to use one section or to remove an unwanted element but they cannot make a poorly focused, dark photo reproduce well in print.

Such photos should not be used. A good designer will suggest an alternative way to create visual interest.

Illustrations can be used instead of photos and sometimes may be preferable. If the editorial is conveying general rather than specific information it may not be possible to obtain a suitable photo but an illustrator could be briefed to provide an appropriate image. Illustrations need not cost more than professional photos. You need to see some examples of an illustrator's work to be sure you are happy about the style. Your designer may be able to recommend someone whose style will be suitable or you could approach your local art college to recommend students or recent graduates willing to undertake freelance work.

The words may also seem easier to read if they are presented in two or three columns rather than running right across the page so that the text seems dense and never-ending. Prominent headings and sub headings should be used to help readers find their way around the document. Some statements can be set in **bold** or *italics* or in a larger type size for emphasis. By introducing such elements the designer creates variety and makes each page look interesting. However the design should not contain so many superfluous devices that it becomes cluttered and fails to achieve the clarity that will assist and attract the reader.

Diagrams, maps and tables of information presented graphically can also provide visual interest. The detailed statistics you must provide in a prospectus can be laid out in various ways. A simple bar chart can be made more interesting and relevant by creating it from a pile of coins or groups of people. A good designer will be able to advise you about the most effective way to present the figures relating to your school's performance, absence rates and so on.

Designers can also create visual interest on a page by lifting a quote from the text and giving it prominence on the page. If you want to highlight something this can be extremely effective.

These two examples illustrate the difference that good composition can make to a photograph. The top example lacks composition and framing, with poor results. The picture on the left has been well grouped, with pleasing results. Attention to technical aspects such as focus and exposure are also important for good results.

Using colour - whether full colour or spot colour (an extra colour other than black) - adds interest and emphasis, but will cost more.

Design

Good design invites people to read the publication by making it visually attractive and interesting. It brings together a number of disparate elements to give the document its distinctive identity. The designer must ensure that the publication is easy to read, using a legible typeface, a typesize that is not too small and laying out the text in manageable sections surrounded by plenty of white space so the reader can easily identify them.

You should provide the designer with as much information as possible at the initial briefing: about your objectives in producing the publication; the amount of text, tables and other material that must be included; how much scope there is for altering the presentation of tables of statistics and other essential information; how many photos or pictures are available - show them to the designer who will be able to assess how useful they will be; what your budget is; how many copies you need printed and any other items of information you think may be useful. The designer will probably ask some questions you have not thought of and will also be able to suggest different types of paper and printing methods that will suit your budget.

By gaining an understanding of your preferences and aims the designer will be better able to put forward a number of preliminary designs to meet your needs. These preliminary designs will give several possibilities for the layout of the entire publication but will simply have spaces marked for pictures and some text shown in one area to give you an impression of the type style and other areas of text roughly pencilled in. However the unifying design elements which pull the publication together will be apparent. Once you have seen these early rough designs you can discuss them with the designer, saying which elements from each you like, or perhaps immediately settling on one design but requiring a few small details to be changed. The designer will then be able to produce the complete design ready for photos and diagrams or graphs to be dropped into the final artwork.

Copy preparation, proof reading and corrections

The designer prepares the artwork to go to the printer. The editor must prepare the copy. Text should be typed double spaced with wide margins to allow room for corrections and typographical instructions. These instructions to the printer indicate the typeface and type size to be used, the measure or width of column across which type is to be set, and any areas to be set in bold, italics or capitals. Any corrections to the text should also be marked. Use red or green pen to mark up the copy as these colours stand out against the typescript. Check whether your printer is willing to receive copy which contains corrections. Some are used to heavily marked up copy, but others prefer clean copy in which case it is best to comply.

Captions to photos and illustrations may be provided on a separate sheet of paper, clearly indicating which page and picture they are associated with. Not every picture needs a caption and the best captions are brief but create a link to the text without repeating what is obvious or is mentioned elsewhere in the text. They should add some relevant interesting information that causes the reader to want to read more about the item depicted.

Once the copy has been set the printer will return it for correction. Proof reading takes time and concentration. The most commonly used proof reading marks are shown on page 96. You need to check every detail - every word, every caption, every headline, every punctuation mark - against the original. You will have to be particularly careful to check that figures have been set accurately. Any corrections which arise from typesetting errors are printer's corrections. If you make changes after typesetting these are author's corrections and you have to pay for them. It is best to mark them in a different colour from the printer's corrections. Better still, avoid them by having perfectly clean copy at the start. In practice you will probably have some author's corrections because it is extremely difficult to 'cast off' the text to exactly fit the page, no matter how carefully you have calculated the length of the text and tried to edit it to fit the available space. So you will probably have to do a small amount of final editing when you see how the typeset words look on the page.

When the printer returns the corrected typesetting, be sure to read complete sentences and paragraphs in case further errors have crept in when corrections were being made. To save time some editors make the final corrections at the printers just before the publication is printed. Here is an example of marked-up copy.

The designer prepares the artwork to go to the printer. The editor must prepare the copy.

run on

Text should be typed double spaced with wide margins to allow room for corrections and typographical instructionsThese instructions to the printer indicate the typeface any indication of areas to be set in bold, italics or capitals. Any corections to the text should also be marked. Use red or green peen to mark up the copy as these colors stand out against the typescript. check whether your printer is willing to to receive copy which contains corrections - some are used too heavily marked-up copy, but others prefer clean copy in which you should comply.

case

Printing

The cost of printing depends on various factors including the type of paper used, the print processes involved, colours used, the finish required, type of binding and length of the print run. Short print runs are more expensive per document printed because of the setting up cost; for each print job the machines have to be prepared with the correct paper and inks. You can ask your designer or a printer to suggest the most suitable materials for your publication, to obtain the effect you want. A printer will give a verbal estimate for a job but this will not necessarily be completely accurate. To obtain a written quotation you will need to prepare a written brief specifying the type(s) of paper to be used for the cover and inside pages, format of the publication - size of page, number of pages, colour(s) to be used, number of copies required, illustrations or photos to be included, any special finishes, method of binding and other detail they may request. This will provide sufficient information for the printer to estimate accurately the cost for the job and provide a binding, written quotation.

Rather than deal directly with the printer yourself you may ask your designer to manage this aspect of the production. The designer will obviously charge an extra fee for this service but this will be worthwhile if the designer is used to dealing with printers and has regular contact with a reliable firm. Ask the designers from whom you seek quotes to show you examples of printed material which they have both designed and seen through the print process. You should obtain written quotations from several designers and printers for the work you wish them to undertake.

Variety of publications

As well as publishing the compulsory prospectus some schools may decide to publish a regular newsletter or a school magazine. The latter can enhance the image and reputation of the school, even though this is not its primary purpose. As with every other

Common proof correction marks (from BS5261, © British Standards Institution)

Instruction	traditional mark	new mark	example of use
insert	λ	λ	insert missing character(s)
delete	♂	♂	delete character or words
italics	———	++++	italicise the underlined word
bold	∿∿∿	∿∿∿	enbolden the marked word
capitals	≡≡≡	≡≡≡	change marked characters to capitals
lower case	/	≢	change capitals to lower case
transpose	⊔	⊔	reverse the order of the characters or words
close up characters	⌣	⌣	remove extra space between
insert space	#/	⅄	add space between words
new paragraph	⌐⌐	⌐⌐	end of paragraph. Start another paragraph
run on (ie no new paragraph.	⌐∼	⌐∼	end of sentence. Continue the paragraph.

The traditional marks are still widely used by printers, the new British Standardhaving been introduced in 1976.

marketing activity, you need to be sure of your objective before going ahead with such publications. The writing and visual style of a school magazine will differ from the style needed in the prospectus, though sometimes you may find photos taken for a school magazine are suitable for the prospectus. Some large companies promote their services by creating videos but this is well beyond the means of the average school and therefore outside the scope of this book.

The prospectus must be updated each year to provide the latest set of statistics but the overall design of the document need not change annually. If a good design has been created which provides the flexibility to insert up-to-date information while retaining much of the material that does not need to change it would be cost effective to use it for several years. After a while a change would be needed and another design should replace it.

The content of a school magazine, on the other hand, must change with each issue. The writing style for news stories, headlines and captions needs to be more like that of a tabloid newspaper than the more formal prose used in the prospectus - not that the more formal approach should be allowed to make the prospectus seem boring. There is also a greater need in a school magazine for a wide variety of pictures, including photos of events being reported on, examples of students' artwork, illustrations and even cartoons. There may be some feature articles on topics of interest to the student community.

The basic design should remain constant, as with a newspaper, so that readers know where to expect news stories, feature articles, and items such as a crossword or the letters page and recognise the overall style. You need to decide how often to publish a school magazine or newsletter and be certain that enough new material will be available for each issue. If the school magazine appears once or twice a year this should be possible but you need

Here are three different styles of school prospectus. The Holy Rood School, Edinburgh, has sold advertising and sponsorship to fund a lavish booklet with a full-colour cover and photographs inside. Monkstown Community School in Northern Ireland has produced a professional-looking brochure, with well-chosen photographs and clear layout. Bradley Rowe Middle School has opted for a simpler style, using a word processor and spiral binding. Available budget may determine what style you choose for your prospectus.

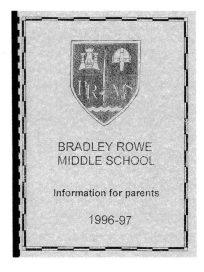

to calculate the design, setting and print cost each time to decide how often the school can afford it.

For a school magazine or newspaper much of the writing and production can be handled by students and if the school has desk top publishing software it can be used to format the pages. Although desktop publishing is feasible for designing and producing a school prospectus, the result will only be satisfactory if the person using the DTP package is both an experienced user and a good designer. As the prospectus is likely to be the school's most prestigious publication it is best not to risk a poor result by having an inexperienced person produce it in this way even though it may seem less expensive. Some economies are not justifiable as part of a successful marketing programme.

Copyright

If you commission written contributions or photos for a school publication then the school owns the copyright. In the case of written material this gives you the right to publish it in the publication for which it was commissioned or in any other suitable publication without having to pay more than the amount you originally paid. Owning the copyright of photos means that the photographer has no right to use your photos elsewhere but, unless you have negotiated a separate fee to buy the negatives, they remain the property of the photographer. Therefore, if you wish to use the photo on future occasions, the photographer is entitled to charge you a fee for additional prints. If you obtain photos from a photo library you will have to pay a fee giving you the right to reproduce the picture; the fee depends on the use you will make of the photo and should be agreed in advance.

Electronic publishing: the Internet

The Internet is a world-wide, interactive network of computer systems that allows people with a computer, modem and telephone line to gain access to the many thousands of pages of information and entertainment 'published' on the Internet. Information can be put on to the Internet by companies, individuals - and schools. Some schools in the UK already have web sites giving information about themselves as part of an IT project.

The marketing potential of the Internet for schools is limited: not many of the people you will wish to reach will have the capability to access the system; and those that do may well be put off by the complicated protocols involved in getting to where you want to be on the Web. However, it would not be wise to ignore these type of developments as the potential for using such systems for marketing purposes will undoubtedly increase as more people routinely gain access to the network, and become used to using it for more than just 'surfing'.

If your school has a teacher with the necessary IT interest and skills he or she may be able to organise projects for certain classes or extra-curricular groups which will create the content and get a school site up and running on the Internet. There will also be a need to keep the information accurate and up to date. Perhaps parents with experience of creating Web sites may be able to help with setting up a site that you will be happy with. The cost of having it done professionally will be prohibitive for most schools, and there will probably be more cost effective ways of spending a marketing budget.

Awareness of the Internet, and of other electronic publishing media, is something that will probably raise the school's profile locally, and being known for being up to date is never a bad thing!

Chapter 9
Events

Every school organises some events. They may be attended by parents, prospective parents, people from the local community or groups from other schools. Events create an impact which is usually far stronger and more memorable than other communication methods, such as advertising, newspaper articles, newsletters or prospectuses. People are more prepared to believe what they see for themselves which is why it is so important to present the school in the best light possible on all such occasions.

The range of events which schools hold includes:
- Parent/Teacher Association meetings
- Parents' evenings or afternoons - when parents meet their children's teachers for a progress report
- Open Days/Evenings - when prospective parents and pupils visit to learn about the school
- School Fairs, Bazaars or Jumble sales - fund raising activities
- School Concerts, Plays and Sports Days
- Speech Days.

Some aspects of event organisation are common to all events, such as publicity. There is no point in organising an event if no-one turns up on the day so good publicity is an essential part of organising any event. A calendar of events should be issued to all parents at the start of the year, and reminders sent before each meeting. If the reminders are sent home by pupil-post they may not be delivered. Ask interested parents at the start of the school year if they would be willing to pay a charge to cover postage for reminders to be sent by mail for the rest of the year - assuming you have a willing publicist. Refer to the chapters on public relations and advertising for more information.

Presentation is also important. The overall appearance of the school in terms of how well the buildings and grounds are maintained and whether they are kept tidy creates a strong impression.

The timing of an event partly determines whether it is successful. If you consider the needs of the majority of people for whom the event is intended, you are more likely to increase the numbers present. If there are a large number of single parents at your school you might consider providing a creche as a way of increasing attendance at PTA meetings. If the school is in an area of high unemployment it may also be preferable to have after-school rather than evening meetings, but if most of your school's parents work then evening meetings would gain a larger audience. You need to consider your staff's needs too.

It is also important to adhere to the published timetable so that people can get away on time, for example if they have baby-sitters waiting at home. This requires a good chair-person or someone to prompt the chair. Meetings should also start on time; this shows efficiency and gets people into the habit of arriving on time.

PTA meetings should address issues of current concern to parents and staff. The agenda should prioritise items for discussion and during the meetings constructive suggestions can be considered and actions proposed and voted on to decide where parental involvement may be useful. The agenda should be published in advance so that parents can make sure they attend if an issue is being discussed about which they feel strongly. Without an agenda and a strong chairperson meetings can become ineffective, and a waste of everyone's time. Staff already have enough to do so are unlikely to be too enthusiastic about PTA meetings which achieve little. Most parents are also busy, so the meeting dates and agenda should be widely publicised well ahead of time.

Parents' evenings

Unlike PTA meetings whose success is as much the responsibility of parents as the school, parents' evenings are definitely the responsibility of the school. They are the opportunity for parents to meet their child's teachers to discuss progress. Parents with an interest in their children's wellbeing are keen to attend such evenings. They may not be so keen to wait in endless queues to see a particular teacher or find that they cannot spend much time with the teacher because by the time they meet the evening is almost at an end. The way such evenings are organised is vital to their smooth running and contributes to parents' overall perception of the school and feelings of satisfaction with it.

Although it is easier to manage an event if fewer people attend, staff should ensure that as many parents as possible come. This will save them having to meet parents at other times and also give them a chance to discuss and perhaps remedy any difficulties, whether the difficulties are experienced by or caused by the child. Supportive parents will almost certainly attend. But you need to attract the other parents as well.

In organising parents' evenings primary schools have an advantage in keeping the queues to a minimum since parents need only meet one teacher who knows all about the pupils in his or her care.

The school should plan for the teacher to meet all parents. Many schools arrange an appointments system to facilitate this.

Secondary schools, sixth form colleges and the like need to provide parents with the opportunity to meet individual subject teachers as well as a form tutor so that they learn about their child's ability in all areas. This presents a greater logistical challenge in organising the event. Using a large enough school hall to accommodate all teachers or at least teachers of core curriculum subjects in one area enables parents to see which teachers are free at any point or where there is only a short queue. They can prioritise their needs and see the teachers they most want to speak to first.

It is important to provide plenty of prominent signs to direct visitors to the correct parts of the building on parents' evenings and at other times.

If non-English speaking parents are expected special arrangements should be made. Your local education authority or council translation service may be able to help.

Many parents have to rush from work to parents' evenings and may be tired and rather hungry, so it is a good idea to provide some refreshment. Tea, coffee, soft drinks and biscuits are sufficient to make them feel welcome. Parents whose children are in other years than those being reviewed can be asked to help serve the teas and if necessary, a charge could be made to help cover the cost.

Open days/evenings

Open days or evenings remain the most effective way of showing the school to a large number of prospective parents and pupils. The school must therefore present itself well. As well as a talk to explain what the school offers, visitors should be given the opportunity to see round the school, escorted by pupils. You need to ensure that the classrooms show a level of activity that impresses. Pupils showing parents around should be confident, friendly and polite. The way in which the school presents itself extends to the appearance of staff and students when they are representing the school and each school needs to decide its own policy on such matters.

The quality of speeches made on formal occasions including open days can influence prospective parents. It is best to keep speeches fairly short and to the point. If you're not the most charismatic speaker ask your deputy and other staff to speak about certain topics. This will give variety and an opportunity to introduce other senior staff so that visitors get a better picture of the school. Allow time for questions.

When preparing for questions you should be aware of current topics, such as league tables or truancy rates, and be prepared to answer specific questions about them. You may need to take action beforehand to show that any problems relating to such areas are being addressed.

School fairs, bazaars and jumble sales

Fund raising events such as school fairs (these may be called bazaars, fetes etc.) and jumble sales take a great deal of organising and need the support of dedicated parents and staff. The PTA usually initiates such events and nominates someone to manage them in association with the head teacher. The events checklist at the end of this chapter will serve as a reminder of many of the tasks associated with this job. Whoever does it will need to put in considerable time and effort to be sure the day is a success but, with the willing collaboration of other parents and staff, such events can be rewarding for the school.

People should be given responsibility for various activities, for example publicity and programmes; arranging stalls, marquees, tables, chairs; raffle (you may need a licence from your local authority); insurance and security (probably the head teacher or delegated staff members); money (usually the PTA treasurer); each stall. Catering for lunches on the day can be a large task and may be divided among different people depending on what is being offered. Various stalls can provide different types of food and drinks to suit different groups, for example savoury snacks which pupils can afford, a baked potato stand, ethnic foods, a selection of salads and cold meats, tea, coffee and cold drinks, and a sweet course such as strawberries and cream in mid-summer. Each would be the responsibility of one person with others helping them.

The event manager would have to work closely with all the individuals responsible for each of these areas, checking on progress, encouraging as many people as possible to volunteer to run a stall or to be involved, and helping to overcome problems along the way. On the day the event manager would ensure that all the items on the programme happened as planned. If the programme said lunches would be served from 12.00 and the raffle drawn at 3.30 announcements would be needed at these times. Someone should be available to make announcements throughout the day. Some theatrical ability on the part of the announcer helps create the right feeling of excitement and enjoyment. Most schools have parents or staff with the necessary flair.

School fairs, bazaars etc. are an opportunity for people in the local community to come into the school. Many will enjoy the entertainment and activities arranged and this can lead to them adopting a favourable view of the school, rather than being neutral or perhaps even hostile to it.

Jumble sales and car boot sales are other methods of raising money. These events do not require the same amount of advance planning as a large school fair but they must be well controlled.

Checklist for organising events

Before the event:
Assign overall responsibility for the event

Publicity	press releases
	advertisements
	posters
	direct mail
	date listing in school calendar issued at start of school year
	letters home
Programme of events	printing
Photography	book and brief photographer for the day
Registration	visitors write name and address at open days (build database for further marketing) and indicate where they heard of the event (as feedback for future publicity)

Theme for event

Guests speakers	invitations
	brief them about their involvement
	arrangements to meet/entertain them during event
Food	who is in charge
	who will prepare food/where
	cooking facilities/utensils
	where and what to serve on plates/cutlery/napkins/tablecloths
	pricing
Drink	who is in charge
	who will provide drinks/glasses/cups etc.
	liquor licence if alcohol served
	water urn/kettles etc. if hot drinks served
	who will sell/what price
Signs	to direct visitors
Arrangements	for speakers of other languages

Escorts	to show people to seats/round school etc.
Name badges	if appropriate for type of event
Presentation	general appearance of the school
	speeches/slides/flip charts/other
	presentation materials
Appointments system	eg. for parents' evenings
Seating arrangements	for special guests
	for other visitors
	for staff
	for pupils
Stalls	hire of stalls, tables, marquees etc.
	assembling and dismantling
	decorating
Entertainment	hire of fun fair items such as bouncy
	castles, merry-go-rounds, etc.
Raffle	permit to hold one
	tickets
	sales
	drawing the raffle/notifying prize
	winners/distributing the prizes
Prizes	obtaining them for raffles, tombola and
	other games - approach local firms for
	donations
	buy and engrave suitable prizes for
	speech days, sports days etc.
Jumble	collecting and sorting
Public address system	PA/Tannoy/microphone/loudspeaker etc.
	plus music - obtaining and testing before
	event
Brief staff	
Rehearsal	as needed
Security and safety	
Insurance	

On the day and after:

Reception desk	if needed, for collecting tickets, selling programmes, registering attendance, displaying leaflets/information packs etc.
Money	providing a float to each person (eg. stall holder, refreshment points, ticket seller) needing one collecting money and replenishing small change throughout the event counting proceeds/keeping accounts/banking
VIPs	special attention

Assign senior person to deal with problems

Letter of thanks to VIPs, people donating prizes etc.

Written report by organiser highlighting things that went well and things to avoid for future similar events (only if it will be filed and used)

Chapter 10
Strategy and
planning

Planning what marketing activities the school will undertake introduces rigour to a process that will be far less effective if activities are carried out on an ad hoc basis in reaction to external circumstances. The marketing plan defines the overall programme of all marketing activities for a specific period. Detailed activities may be planned for the year ahead and an outline of anticipated activities for the following two or four years added to show longer term plans.

Preparing a marketing plan should not happen in isolation. It should be part of the school's complete planning cycle. The person responsible for marketing will need to be aware of the overall objectives for the school in order to ensure that marketing objectives fit in with them. Otherwise a marketing plan could have growth as its objective when the school's overall objective is to keep numbers constant and improve educational provision, in which case the marketing plan should focus on improvement.

Marketing plans should be based on strategies devised to meet the school's objectives. For example, if a school's overall objective is to maintain current numbers but research has shown that the school age population in the immediate area is dwindling, the strategy might be extending the school's catchment area while maintaining its position within its existing area. Plans for various types of marketing activity based on this strategy would be prioritised and costed so that lower priority items could be dropped if the overall budget would not accommodate everything.

It is obvious from the above example that the precursor to setting objectives is an audit and an analysis of the strengths, weaknesses, opportunities and threats it reveals.

The planning process consists of the sequence of activities outlined below.

Marketing audit

A marketing audit should be performed to provide the information needed to decide objectives, just as audits should be carried out for other functions such as teaching, finance and administration to assess the school's overall performance.

SWOT

By using the information from the audit to assess strengths and weaknesses in all areas, including marketing, it becomes possible to set realistic achievable objectives which address current needs.

Objectives

The headteacher, senior management and governors of the school may all be jointly involved in setting objectives for the school, based on an audit of the whole school. These must be communicated to people with responsibility for every function within the school so that they can develop plans aligned with overall objectives. The person responsible for the school's marketing will need to take into account both the overall school objectives and the results of a SWOT analysis based on the marketing audit in order to set marketing objectives.

Objectives should be measurable, for example, to maintain student numbers this year and increase numbers by five per cent within three years. The key to setting marketing objectives is matching your school (the product) to the needs of the market.

The objectives for each individual marketing function, such as public relations, advertising and brochure production, would have to be related to this overall objective, stressing academic improvements and success.

Strategy

Strategy is the means by which you expect to achieve the school's objectives in a particular area. For example to achieve the objective of increasing school numbers the most suitable strategy may be to improve academic standards within the school. Alternatively, if your market is already crowded with schools that are academically excellent you may choose a marketing strategy that focuses on the range of vocational courses your school offers or its sporting and extra curricular provision. Plans based on such a strategy could be devised to attract students whose interests and abilities are not met by your competitors. They could position the school as a centre of excellence for vocational or sports education. This need not preclude continued efforts to improve academic standards too.

Strategies can be changed if they are found to be less effective than expected when put into practice. However, in pursuing a long term strategy it takes time to effect change and even more time to undo it if it proves to be wrong. Therefore it is advisable to test the suitability of a strategy (perhaps by conducting some research within one of the feeder primary schools) before you decide to embark on it.

Plans

The detailed plans for each marketing function should identify specific tactics based on the marketing strategy for that function. Strategy is conceptual and qualitative in scope but tactics must be measurable. They will give quantitative information such as numbers to be achieved, resources needed, costs and time scales.

Measurement

You should periodically review your marketing plan to check progress toward your objectives. Was the estimated budget adequate for what was planned or is it running out? Have some activities taken longer than expected or been completed with time to spare? Priorities should be revised in the light of this review.

You should also assess how successful various types of marketing activity have proved. For example, advertising the school open day in a wider range of papers than previously may not have increased numbers attending as much as you had hoped, or an increase may have occurred for some other reason. Unless you devise methods for measuring the success of your marketing activities you will have no way of knowing which are best to pursue in future. This information should be fed back into the planning process.

Many businesses formally review their plans every month. Staff responsible for each function provide a financial report and progress summary to senior management, which is the basis for agreeing any changes that are needed. Without this information senior management would be unable to control the business.

Schools should use similar procedures to review their marketing progress, priorities and budget, though school terms and holidays may dictate a different reporting cycle.

The planning process

At any point in the planning process it is worth involving people who may make a valuable contribution. You could have help in conducting the audit, performing the SWOT analysis, defining objectives and planning activities within each marketing function. The final plan should be a written one so that it can be reviewed throughout the year.

If you plan and write down the plan in accord with the sequence of activities mentioned above, from marketing audit through to measurement, you will do a professional job. It doesn't matter if the writing consists largely of introductory paragraphs, bullet point actions and reasons for including them, provided there is a record of the plans, why decisions have been made, methods of measurement to be used and costs. You need to specify who is responsible for each activity, who has overall responsibility and what systems will support the marketing team.

Marketing programme for XYZ School - 1996

Responsibility for marketing:

Background

mention items from marketing audit such as:
- economy of area - unemployment
- legislation affecting school - eg. opportunity to opt out of LEA control under consideration
- social/cultural mix in the intake area
- trends in local population
- size of market and expected growth/contraction

The school

teaching quality, exam results in various curriculum areas buildings (state of repair/overall appearance
facilities, equipment, resources for humanities, science, music, art, languages, IT, sports, library etc.
school management

student support
location and transport
recruitment

membership of trade associations

Competition
other schools - what is known about each in terms of marketing
ability, educational performance etc.
links with other schools

Detail of the school's marketing activities and systems
market research
product development (ie. changes to the school)
advertising
public relations
brochures
events
customer service

general comments on the school's current marketing system eg
objectives, responsibilities, information systems/ controls, cost
effectiveness - these will affect plans for the coming year as they
may have to be put in place or improved

SWOT analysis

Strengths	Weaknesses
Opportunities	Threats

Marketing objectives

State what you do to match your school to the market in terms of the school as it is (existing product for existing market), as it may be (new product for existing market), as it is for an extended market (existing product for new market) or as it may be far an extended market (new product for new market). Ensure the objectives have measurement built in.

Marketing strategies

identify strategy to achieve above objectives in terms of
  product change (ie. changes in the school)
  promotion - (PR, advertising, events, brochures etc.)

Plans based on strategies
  for changes in the schools
  for promotional activities

Measurement
    of progress toward objectives (feedback methods - may need to include implementing marketing systems in the overall objectives/plan)
    of change in the school
    of individual promotional activities
  Mention measurement techniques to be used in each case.

Finally...

The content of this book has covered a wide range of marketing activities. They should be regarded as an ideal. The reality is that most schools will probably only be able to use some of the suggestions. However if the book gives you a new insight into marketing, causes you to try some new techniques and improve others, it will have achieved its objective of helping your school in an area that is new to most teachers. Good luck in using your newly acquired knowledge to market your school.